PAGANISM FOR BEGINNERS

PAGANISM
FOR BEGINNERS

The Complete Guide to Nature-Based

Spirituality for Every New Seeker

ALTHAEA SEBASTIANI

callisto
publishing
an imprint of Sourcebooks

Copyright © 2020 by Callisto Publishing LLC
Cover and internal design © 2020 by Callisto Publishing LLC
Interior & Cover Designer: Erik Jacobsen
Art Producer: Janice Ackerman
Editor: Sean Newcott
Production Editor: Rachel Taenzler
Author photo courtesy of Athaea Sebastiani

Published by Callisto Publishing LLC C/O Sourcebooks LLC
P.O. Box 4410, Naperville, Illinois 60567-4410
(630) 961-3900
callistopublishing.com

Printed and bound in China
OGP 2

To the one person who proved their willingness to wrestle a bear for me by putting up with my nonsense on a daily basis

CONTENTS

INTRODUCTION

HAIL THE SEEKER! And welcome to the beginning of a journey of spiritual exploration and discovery. Together, we'll be delving beneath the umbrella of modern Paganism to gain a deeper understanding of the dominant values, characteristics, and practices of this religious movement, as well as exploring many of its individual traditions. Although modern, Paganism owes much to the past—for inspiration and for the trailblazing individuals who laid its groundwork. The highly adaptable nature of Paganism is largely due to its ability to keep a foot in the past with eyes on the future, allowing it to bend, flex, and expand to meet the needs of a modern people.

In a time when it is easy to feel disconnected from everything—including yourself—Paganism provides a means for you to regain that connection, to reclaim wholeness, and to see the world in a new way that rejects disillusionment and, instead, replaces it with wonder, depth, and meaning. It's that connection and wholeness that draws many to Paganism and is why Paganism continues to be one of the fastest-growing religious movements in the world.

Each of us comes to Paganism from a variety of backgrounds for a unique reason. In truth, there are no two Pagans who are alike in experience and personal practice, although we share many similarities that bring us together as a community. This diversity is a source of strength in the Pagan community and why we are each actively encouraged to find our own way within this movement, choosing our practices, our traditions, and even our Gods based on what we need to help us grow and become better people.

My own journey into Paganism began when I was a young child. Like for many people, it was a path of progression that, in hindsight, almost seems fated.

I grew up on my grandparents' farm nestled at the end of a dead-end dirt road in rural northern Wisconsin. All too often I was left to my own devices and frequently roamed the forests and fields, a handful of barn cats diligently following after me.

We grew or hunted most of our food. The looming threat of a harsh northern winter meant that the warm months were dominated by family gatherings. Every aunt, uncle, and cousin would return to the family farm to attend to the harvest—be it hay, corn, deer, chickens, pigs, or firewood—that would be necessary to get through the months of snow and ice. Our existence was pulled from the land, and I knew from early on that the world was much larger than I heard it described. I knew that there was more about the land and the idea of God than I was told was possible to experience. There were hints of this everywhere, in the way the howl of the wind through the trees in the dead of winter would stop my grandfather in his tracks, in the birth of every new calf that would bring the whole family into the barn to watch in silence, and in the way my grandmother would curse in Polish at the spirit in the barn to leave the lights on until we were done milking the cows.

Nourished on a healthy diet of farm superstitions, a belief in spirit, and folklore, I wasn't surprised when I began to see the spirits that shared my family's farm with us, when I began to hear plants whisper secrets that I would later confirm in books on herbalism. Guided by folklore, strong intuition, and the whispers of the land, I developed a functional witchcraft practice by the age of 11, but it would be many years before I would learn that other witches existed and that there were religions that would both welcome and celebrate my practice.

My commitment to a spiritual and Earth-centric experience caused me to break with the religion in which I was raised. Then and now, I bear it no hard feelings. My experience with my family's religion had only been positive, but it didn't align with my reality. Remarkably, an insightful conversation with the pastor of my family's church taught me about animism. Using my spirit-led witchcraft practice as a starting point, I began to search for something that embraced the animism that described my worldview.

Soon, Paganism appeared in my research, and I knew that I was on to something. There were so many similarities between it and the values that had been impressed upon me as a child. It was a natural choice to turn my attention there, one that has served me well and deepened my spiritual practice in all the ways I hoped for as a dirty farm kid with pockets full of twigs and stones.

Through Paganism, I found answers for my experiences and tools to make better sense of them and embrace them. Through Paganism, I found Gods Whose presence in my life would leave me forever changed—stronger, more self-reliant, and with a conviction to speak more freely about my practice so others could more readily find the answers they seek. It is my hope, dear reader, that this book will help you find truth where confusion had once been and that this truth inspires you to meet whatever challenges you may face in your spiritual journey with your head held high—and the Gods at your side.

CHAPTER 1

Understanding Paganism

Paganism is a religious movement comprised of numerous traditions and individual paths. These sometimes wildly varying traditions find common ground in strong values, shared history, and an Earth-centric spiritual ethos. In this chapter, we'll explore some of the movement's defining values and dominant characteristics, and we'll touch on its sweeping history.

The Pagan Movement

The Pagan movement is altogether modern, yet its beginning is rooted in events stretching back several hundred years. Consider the way a barren field will slowly be reclaimed by the wild: Patches of grass and wildflowers appear first, breaking up hard soil and allowing the seeds of woody shrubs and trees to take root and grow in a protected environment. In time, the field will have birthed a forest. It is in this same way that a receptive environment was created for the Pagan movement, with the first seeds planted sometime during the Renaissance (1300–1600) with the discovery of the writings attributed to Hermes Trismegistus and the birth of Western esotericism.

Further seeds were planted during the Romantic movement (1770–1850) with a rise in folklore published specifically for the general public, as well as the creation of the first modern religious Druidry groups (1840s). This momentum was carried forward with the Spiritualist movement beginning in 1848. With a focus on communication with the dead and psychic abilities, divination tools such as Tarot and talking boards took hold in the public's imagination.

Several occult orders and new religious movements were also formed then, such as Theosophy by Helena Petrovna Blavatsky (1875), the Ordo Templi Orientis by Carl Kellner (1895), and Thelema by Aleister Crowley (1904). Also significant was the publication of *Aradia, or the Gospel of the Witches* by Charles Godfrey Leland in 1899. (Leland claimed to have found practicing witches in Italy, and this book was a compilation of their spells and rituals.)

A half a century later in 1951, the repeal of the Witchcraft Act in Britain was a catalyzing event that saw the creation of modern witchcraft by Gerald Gardner. His work was inspired by Leland and Crowley, who coined the spelling of *magick* to distinguish it from illusory stage magic. Gardner called this witchcraft religion *Wicca* and did much to popularize it through actively initiating new members who would spread its reach (such as Raymond Buckland, who brought Wicca to the US in 1964) and also promoting it through the media, capitalizing on public interest and his eccentricity. However, it would be his first high priestess, Doreen Valiente, who would largely rewrite the rituals and lore of Wicca, bringing cohesion and poetry to the work.

Numerous factors contributed to the rising interest in Wicca during the fifties, sixties, and seventies. The work of archaeologist Margaret Murray, though scorned by her peers, was instrumental in propagating the idea that ancient European and Mediterranean peoples worshiped one singular Great Goddess and that there existed an ancient and widespread European witch cult. This idea, even without substantiation, caught hold with the general public and was largely believed into the nineties.

Surging interest in Hinduism and Buddhism in the West further influenced the developing Pagan movement and created an air of acceptance among the general public. Growing interest in feminism and eco-activism also promoted this attitude, as ideas of a Great Goddess and sacred nature appealed to both. The 1979 publication of *Drawing Down the Moon* by Margot Adler would depict a rich and diverse Pagan community and assemblage of traditions stretching across the US.

During the seventies and eighties, the Pagan movement became increasingly diverse with the beginning of polytheistic reconstructionist traditions. These traditions emphasized restoring the polytheistic religions of ancient cultures—such as the Greeks with Hellenism, the Germanic and Norse peoples with Ásatrú, and the ancient Egyptians with Kemeticism.

But it wouldn't be until the nineties that the Pagan movement would establish itself as a firm part of modern religion, thanks to mainstream media interest, increased Internet accessibility, and new books focused on solitary practice (this term refers both to those who practice as "solitaries," i.e., on their own, and to anyone's personal practice, i.e., how they practice Paganism outside of any groups to which they may belong). Today, members of the Pagan movement can be found on nearly every continent and practice a Paganism that is rich and vibrant, encompassing myriad individual traditions and solitary practices. While it can sometimes seem as if there is little in common among these traditions, shared history and a view of the natural world as sacred are the binding glue that bring them together as one Pagan community.

Defining Paganism

As a term, *Pagan* comes to us from the Latin *paganus*, referring to someone who lived in a village or rural area as opposed to a city (*paganus* is derived from the noun *pagus*, meaning village). While the term would be used to differentiate civilians from Roman soldiers for a short while, it was with the rise of Christianity that the term became used for those who maintained their indigenous practices and beliefs. The term *Pagan* is still used, in a pejorative manner, by some Christians to refer to anyone who is not a member of their religion and, sometimes, not a member of their denomination within that religion.

The term acquired new connotations in the late nineteenth and early twentieth centuries, becoming associated with a connection to the past (especially ancient knowledge), self-indulgence, and the sacredness of nature. This would influence the adoption of the term in the sixties to define the Pagan movement, which, then and now, presented itself as an alternative solution to the spiritual questions and needs people faced that were not being sufficiently answered by traditional religions.

It continues to be an umbrella term for the numerous traditions and paths that, while appearing quite different on the surface, all find common ground within Paganism. Yet the term "Pagan" as a religious descriptor is not equally embraced. Many Pagans prefer the term "Neo-Pagan," emphasizing the revivalist and inspired stance that modern Paganism has regarding ancient European religions as well as differentiating it from pre-Christian European religions. Others prefer the term "Heathen," although this term is most frequently used by those practicing Ásatrú, Norse Paganism, or other reconstructions of Norse and Germanic peoples pre-Christian religions. The word "eclectic" is also commonly used (i.e., eclectic Pagan) to denote that an individual's practice is unique to themselves, having been pieced together from bits and pieces of various Pagan traditions. Then there are those who refer to themselves and their practices solely by their tradition's name, such as Wicca or Druidry.

When you are first beginning to explore Paganism, it is completely fine to simply call yourself Pagan. As you grow, study, and become more comfortable within your spiritual practice, you may find specific terms and traditions that appeal to you more, perhaps aligning with your current beliefs or offering you opportunities for growth and learning. It's okay to change your focus from one tradition to another, and it's completely okay to change what you call yourself and your path if that name more accurately represents your beliefs and practices. Such exploration and change are encouraged within Paganism, as it reflects the spiraling nature of life, respects the autonomy of the individual, and underscores personal responsibility for one's practice—all of which are important Pagan values.

As you explore Paganism and its many traditions, perhaps finding local groups and organizations, you'll likely notice a lack of distinct organizational structure. Unlike mainstream religion, Paganism does not have a central organizing body. Even Pagan traditions are loosely organized, with each group within a tradition being autonomous and self-governing. Paired with the sometimes greatly differing practices among traditions and groups, this can make it feel as if Paganism is disjointed and lacking cohesion. But where other religions maintain commonality through shared beliefs and creeds, Pagans find commonality in shared values and worldviews. Pagans frequently take pride in the lack of large-scale organization, as it is more reflective of organizational structures found in nature and allows the greatest individual religious freedom and expression. We are, if nothing else, a community of individuals—much like single cells that willingly and joyfully come together to form a larger organism. We are a community that embraces a shared vision of communities strong in their love for—and protection of—a world imbued with divinity.

The Pagan Way

Although each tradition speaks for itself, there are commonalities in practice, values, and worldview that can be witnessed among individual Pagans. Embracing these values, as well as others, is a defining part of being Pagan. Let's explore these standards in more detail.

Blessedness

To bless something is to call upon the Divine to imbue that thing with Their power and favor. Pagans believe that you naturally possess the favor of the Gods and that They are inclined to respond favorably to your worship. Pagans also believe that the Earth, the universe, and all of nature are also inherently predisposed to Divine favor and are intrinsically sacred. Pagans don't view people or the world as flawed or in need of saving. Our natural state at birth and throughout life is one of being inherently sacred, worthy, and blessed. This inextricable sacredness of all the physical world—including the people in it—fills Pagan practice with a joyful wonder for life and living.

Clergy and Religious Specialists

There is nothing that stands between you and the Gods; everyone is capable of approaching and honoring Them with assurance that you are capable of receiving a response. Yet Paganism recognizes the need for clergy and other religious specialists. Clergy and specialists undergo additional training that allows them to provide valuable services because of their expertise. They may also hold certifications and licenses that allow them to perform legally recognized services, such as officiating weddings and offering spiritual counseling.

Holistic Worldview

One of the things that makes Paganism so relevant in modern times is that as much as it embraces a spiritual view of the world, it also embraces a *scientific* one. This adds a multilayered approach in regard to how Pagans interact with and view the world, as there is no incompatibility between our religious traditions and the latest scientific discoveries. Many Pagans find that science provides a means of deepening their understanding of the universe, which allows them to feel a stronger connection to the Earth, the Gods, and each other.

Inclusivity

The Pagan movement is open to all who desire to be Pagan. There is no discrimination based on gender, sexuality, race, age, or ability. In recognizing that all life is sacred, Pagans recognize that all *people* are sacred. Diversity is one of the greatest strengths in nature, ensuring species populations are able to thrive, and so diversity within the members of the Pagan community is viewed as a strength. Diversity helps local communities remain responsive and flexible. It also helps each of us, on an individual level, remain focused on living our values.

Integrity

This is how we embody Pagan values in our everyday lives. It's how we walk our talk, how we ensure that our religious practices touch us on that deep level that encourages spiritual and personal growth. It's so easy to get distracted by the tedium of your life, but a focus on integrity encourages us to make time for the things that mean the most to us, even if that means only being able to spend a few minutes each day at our altar or communing with the Gods outside. The point is that you try, that you act, that your life reflects those values and beings you hold dear.

Interconnectedness

An underlying element of the Pagan worldview is that all things are bound and connected. Many Pagans view this connection as existing on an energetic level—all things contain and are made of energy, and this energy is the same within us all. It is through this interconnection that magick is made possible, such as when healing magick is worked for a friend going through surgery. Interconnection also bids you to be more aware of the consequences of your actions, as they do not affect you alone.

Freedom of Choice

Paganism does not possess a central hierarchy—it generally takes a polytheistic view of deities, recognizing a multitude of Gods and Goddesses. Each of us is free to honor whichever deities we choose, building strong relationships with Them. Because of this diversity of personal religious expression, it is only natural that Paganism professes no dogma. There are no inarguable codes of conduct, no divinely inspired texts, nothing that isn't open for question and debate. This is further evidenced in the lack of governing bodies and central religious figures. As a Pagan, you are free to determine the details of your practice.

Personal Responsibility

With no governing texts or officials, it comes down to each of us to ensure that we are holding to our values, giving the Gods due honor, and living with integrity. There is no fear of divine punishment in life or after death. Rather, there are consequences for your actions—as true in your everyday life as it is in your spiritual life—and a need for you to each hold yourself accountable. Pagans take note of their mistakes and faults, and they strive to do better, to be better. We acknowledge our mistakes, and we do what we can to rectify them.

Religion

Although there is a strong emphasis on personal freedom, Paganism encourages you to approach your practices as rightful religions. There is little in the way of orthodoxy (i.e., what you should believe in order to be Pagan) to guide your seeking, yet through the experiences you gain in performing rituals, honoring the Gods, acknowledging the sacred around you, and contemplating the interconnectedness of all, many of us come to similar conclusions regarding life's big questions. Religiosity through experience guides us.

Spirituality

In accordance with the theme of diversity so prominent within Paganism, every Pagan's spiritual practice will be unique to them. This practice can encompass many different things, with no set combination or minimum of things required to be Pagan. Spiritual practice frequently involves ritual, meditation, divination, magick, and communication with Gods and spirits—but these practices are often embodied, such as through singing, chanting, dancing, consensual intimacy, and music.

Pagan by Law

W hile the United States government does not officially recognize any religion, Paganism and all of its traditions are entitled to, and protected by, the same protections afforded mainstream religions. The First Amendment to the Constitution secures the freedom of religious practice for all citizens, while Section One of the Fourteenth Amendment guarantees those rights by securing equal protection under the law and prohibiting religious discrimination.

Numerous court cases, as well as policies established by the Department of Defense, serve as legal precedent for the recognition of Paganism as a religion by government agencies and bodies. For example, in 1986, *Dettmer v. Landon* recognized Wicca, a Pagan tradition, as entitled to First Amendment protection specifically in regard to incarcerated Pagans; however, it did not rule that prohibiting Wiccan ritual tools was unconstitutional. This was the first time that any Pagan tradition would receive legal recognition. In 2007, the US military approved the pentacle (the symbol of Wicca) on government-issued gravestones; in 2013, it approved Thor's hammer (aka Mjölnir, the symbol of Ásatrú); and in 2017, the awen (the symbol of Druidry).

Legal recognition and protection can vary greatly in other countries. For example, while Canada does not officially recognize or give status to any religion, there are no Pagan charities that carry legal recognition. This can lead to complications in securing religious protection under the law. In the United Kingdom, Paganism is recognized by the National Board of Religion, with the Pagan Federation and the Druid Network being recognized Pagan charitable organizations. Australia does not officially recognize any religion, but its lower population presents a significant challenge for the small Pagan populace to form a sizable-enough organization to warrant recognition as a religious institution.

CHAPTER 2
Pagan Paths

Many different forms of Paganism exist, and they are known as traditions. Each of these traditions is unique; however, some similarities can be seen among them due to shared history. While values and worldview are frequently similar, it is in a tradition's specific focus and ritual practice that the defining details are found and the beauty of that tradition is revealed.

The Traditions of Paganism

A standard among these traditions is a lack of proselytizing. Members come to each tradition of their own accord, as Pagans recognize that everyone's spiritual journey is unique to them—and what works for one of us most certainly cannot work for all of us, as everyone has their own spiritual needs and predispositions. Many Pagans belong to more than one tradition, and their personal practice may look considerably different from any group practice with which they are involved. On the pages that follow, we'll look at some of the most common Pagan traditions.

African Diasporic Religions (ADRs)

Also called African Traditional Religions and African Derived Religions, these religions and traditions have members who do not always consider themselves Pagan, but there are members who are initiated into one (or more) ADR religions and comfortably practice Paganism as well. ADRs are defined by their ties to African deities, mythology, and spiritual practices such as divination, dance, spiritism, and healing. These religions originated primarily throughout the Caribbean and Brazil as a spiritual response from enslaved individuals from Africa. Melding their indigenous beliefs and customs with the Christianity forced upon them, new religions were born that provided new tools to help them cope and survive.

While these religions have spread throughout the world (for example, New Orleans's Voodoo is unique to that locale), they have largely managed to maintain structural integrity with a clear hierarchy of religious specialists and training. The following are some of the major ADRs, along with where they originated or are practiced by large numbers of people:

Candomblé in Brazil

Umbanda in Brazil

Espiritismo in Puerto Rico

Santería (Regla de Ocha, Regla Lucumí, or just Lucumí) in Cuba, the Dominican Republic, and Puerto Rico

María Lionza's religion in Venezuela and the Canary Islands

Shango religion in Trinidad and Grenada

Vodun in Haiti

Alexandrian Wicca

Bearing the name of its founder, Alex Sanders, Alexandrian Wicca is an initiatory coven-based form of Wicca. Although Alexandrian Wicca is based upon Gardnerian Wicca (as Sanders was an initiate), an initially dubious origin story paired with Sanders's own desire for notoriety birthed a unique tradition with a stronger focus on Western esotericism, such as ceremonial and Enochian magic, and original variations on tool use and the deities honored.

Its covens are hierarchical, led by a high priest and high priestess who hold the third and highest degree of initiation (this coven structure is typical for British Traditional Wicca, but *covens* as a type of group are specific to witchcraft and not ubiquitous to Paganism). Depending on the coven, seekers may be permitted to attend a ritual (generally private) prior to initiation into the first degree—which is required to be a part of this tradition.

Within British Traditional Wiccan traditions—which include Alexandrian and Gardnerian Wicca, among other traditions—coven membership is organized into three degrees, each requiring an initiation ceremony in which new information, such as oathbound lore and rituals, is presented to the initiate. First-degree initiation marks entrance into the coven and tradition, as well as becoming part of the priesthood of that coven's deities. Second-degree initiation typically marks being able to teach the tradition and lead rituals. Third-degree is the highest degree and marks individuals who are able to form and lead their own covens within the tradition.

Celtic Polytheism

The term "Celtic" refers to European ethnic groups distinguished by similar languages. This includes people such as the Irish, Scottish, Welsh, and Gauls. Celtic polytheism is a tradition focused on the deities and mythologies of these peoples, frequently focusing on a specific subset (such as Gaulic polytheism), but generally focused on pre-Christian Irish polytheistic religion. For this, there is no formal structure or standard texts. Most members are solitary and rely upon their ability to research in order to develop a deeper understanding of the cultural environment (and views) in which Celtic deities originated.

Some Celtic polytheists are focused on a revivalist and/or reconstructionist approach, attempting to recreate as accurately as possible the religious customs of ancient Celtic peoples. Others are classically inspired and adapt their research to fit the nuances of current times.

Some of the deities that Celtic polytheists may form relationships with include Brighid, Lugh, Epona, Cernunnos, Ceridwen, the Mórrígan, and Danu.

Ceremonial Magic

Playing an integral role in the formation of modern Paganism, ceremonial magic is sometimes referred to as high magick to differentiate it from the style of magick practiced in witchcraft (which is then referred to as low magick).

Although both ceremonial magic and witchcraft work with spirits, there is a distinct difference in approach, as ceremonial magic focuses on conjuring angels, demons, and other spirits within a Christian cosmology and freely makes use of intoning names of the Christian God. Witchcraft, on the other hand, is inherently secular and approaches spirits from an animistic stance.

While the magick worked may focus on improving the quality of one's life, it typically focuses on techniques and exercises for attaining godhead—that is, to fill the individual with the essence and qualities of the Christian God so as to make the individual more godly. This contrasts with witchcraft, where the focus of magick is exclusively on creating change within the everyday; spiritual changes and growth are consequential to the work of the witch but are not the goal of witchcraft. Ceremonial magic is also founded upon strict adherence to ceremony and ritual preparation prior to ritual workings (such preparation can last for days or weeks).

Ceremonial magic is part of, and sometimes used as an alternate name for, Hermeticism and Western esotericism as a whole. It is practiced by solitaries as well as in established groups, such as the Ordo Templi Orientis and the Hermetic Order of the Golden Dawn.

Dianic Wicca

Founded in 1971 by Zsuzsanna Budapest, Dianic Wicca is also known as Dianic Witchcraft and Dianic Feminist Wicca. It is unique among traditions of Wicca, because it is grounded in second-wave feminism and is not polytheistic, as it exclusively honors a goddess (referred to as "the Goddess") and does not recognize male deities. There is no specific goddess honored; rather, all goddesses throughout time and across cultures are viewed as being one.

Controversy surrounds Dianic Wicca within the Pagan community, as it is not inclusive and adamantly opposes allowing men to participate, forbidding their initiation and viewing them as "women's children." Dianic Wicca also prohibits the initiation and inclusion of trans women, stating that they are a tradition solely for "women-born-women" to honor women's mysteries. These mysteries focus on the spiritual significance of reproduction, menstruation, and childbirth as experienced by individuals with uteri. Dianic Wiccans abide by the Wiccan Rede and the Threefold Law and celebrate the Wheel of the Year.

Druidry

Druidry is entirely modern and does not hold a connection to ancient Druids except through inspiration. Although early resurgences of Druidry were Christian, modern Druidry is polytheistic. Exact beliefs will vary from member to member, as well as between larger Druidic organizations (such as Ár nDraíocht Féin and the Order of Bards, Ovates, and Druids). There is no specific pantheon or group of deities honored; however, Irish deities are a common focus among Druids.

Music and culture are highly regarded among Druids, who view poetry, music, and art as inspired by *awen*, a spiritual force that serves as muse and creative generator. Awen is also a symbol representing modern Druidry, depicted as three rays descending vertically. Druids place great significance on the natural world, especially trees, and seek to live in harmony with nature. Druidry can be practiced as a solitary or as part of groups known as "groves."

Eclectic

Many individuals and even groups within Paganism are eclectic. This means that their practice, unique to them, is not part of a larger tradition. Instead, it has been formed from multiple Pagan traditions and religions.

Most modern Pagans are eclectic, learning and exploring their religion through books, online sources, trial and error, participation in occasional community gatherings, and perhaps courses and workshops offered online or in person by teachers and elders in the Pagan community.

Family Traditions

Although there are a few family traditions that can legitimately claim to hold beliefs and practices reaching back several generations, most family traditions are relatively new. But considering that modern Paganism has had a strong presence for around 50 years in the US alone, it is to be expected that many Pagans would raise their children in their beliefs and practices, and that some of those children, once grown, would raise their own children in the same, or similar, beliefs and practices.

These family traditions typically feature a strong appreciation for the natural world, the use of folk magic, and various forms of divination. Joining a family tradition is difficult, as it is the tradition of that family. Members are born into it, marry into it, or (rarely) share their ways with close friends of the family.

Gardnerian Wicca

Named after its founder, Gerald Gardner, Gardnerian Wicca is the oldest form of Wicca. This tradition began in 1939, when Gardner was initiated into a coven of witches in the New Forest district of England. With significant help from his first high priestess, Doreen Valiente, Gardner would build upon the folk customs these witches provided to create a distinct ritual structure and mythos.

This tradition operates in groups called covens, requiring initiation to participate. Rituals are aligned to the Wheel of the Year and lunar cycle and conducted skyclad (naked). Each coven holds to the tradition created by Gardner and Valiente, yet is autonomous and run by a high priestess.

In seeking a Gardnerian coven, keep in mind that many covens are not looking for new members. Those that are will frequently have an Outer Court that provides teaching in witchcraft and an opportunity for you to see whether they are a good fit for you and you for them.

Heathenry

This tradition is also referred to as Ásatrú, and its members may refer to themselves as Heathens or Ásatruár and focus on the pre-Christian religious practices and deities of the Norse and Germanic peoples. This tradition is polytheistic and may be practiced in groups (known as kindreds), individually, or as a hearth-focused tradition, centered upon family and the home.

Rituals are called blóts and center upon the giving of offerings and libations to the Gods. This may be followed by a symbel, where the Gods are toasted and a communal drink is shared. Seiðr, a form of magick, divination, and spiritism, is viewed as a matter for specialists. Women specialists are known as vǫlva or seiðkona (seiðr woman), while men are called seiðmaðr (seiðr man). Women typically practice seiðr more than men, as was traditional in ancient times.

Prominent deities in Heathenry include Odin, Thor, Freyja, Loki, and Tyr.

Hellenic or Greek Polytheism

With a focus on the deities of ancient Greece, Hellenic polytheists may be reconstructionists, attempting to revive and reestablish the religious customs and practice of ancient Greeks; or they may be classically inspired, basing their practices on the mythology, rituals, and practices of ancient Greeks but modifying those practices to more easily fit within their lives.

A few larger organizations exist; however, most Hellenic polytheists practice as solitaries or within their families. Some established groups call themselves "demos" and adhere to the Athenian calendar in honoring the Gods through festivals and feast days. The exact format of worship varies, but it typically entails calling to the Gods and making offerings and libations, which may be burned, buried, or deposited outside.

Typically, a multitude of deities are honored, but some Hellenic polytheists will focus on building deep relationships with a handful of deities. Some of the most commonly honored deities include Zeus, Hera, Artemis, Apollo, Hekate, Hermes, Demeter, and Athena.

Kemeticism

Kemeticism ranges from an eclectic Pagan practice with a focus on Egyptian deities to reconstructionism and an effort to recreate ancient Egyptian religious practice and beliefs as authentically as possible. While many Kemetics practice individually or in family groups, large organizations do exist, such as the House of Netjer, which is also known as Kemetic Orthodoxy.

Kemeticism is largely polytheistic; however, many practitioners are henotheists, meaning that while they believe in the existence of many individual deities and see Them each as worthy of praise and worship, these individuals focus primarily on one deity. For many henotheists, this relationship is similar in level of devotion and love to that of Bhakti in Hinduism.

Spiritual practice includes the observation of several festivals every month, making offerings to various deities, and adherence to Ma'at, a concept that embodies the values of truth, balance, and justice.

Shamanism

Modern shamanism is distinct from indigenous shamanic religions yet is based upon perceived underlying principles shared among them. The worldview of the shaman is that the world is alive with spirits and that the boundary between the physical world and the spirit world can be traversed through ritual and journey work. Such journeying may be done to speak with specific spirits and/or deities, to gain knowledge, or for soul retrieval—a shamanic healing technique that restores health to a person by returning fragmented pieces of the person's spirit to them.

Shamans generally are solitary and frequently are part of other traditions, as shamanic elements can be found within many Pagan traditions. Personal experience, explicit belief in the reality of the spirit world, and the mysteries of nature are hallmarks of modern shamanism.

Solitaries

Many Pagans practice alone, as solitaries. These solitary practitioners frequently have eclectic practices, sometimes building intricate personal philosophies and practices from aspects of various traditions and religions. Solitary Pagans may also adhere to the guidelines of a tradition, such as Wicca, Druidry, or Heathenry, as closely as they can. Solitary Pagans may choose to practice alone due to personal preference, limitations due to family and work obligations, or because they have yet to find a local group that sufficiently meets their needs for spiritual community.

Solitary Pagans will frequently engage with the larger Pagan community through a variety of means, including social media, online groups, large festivals, meetups and moots, and conventions.

Stregheria

As a modern American Pagan witchcraft tradition, Stregheria is inspired by Italian folk magic and ancient Etruscan religion. Much of the material of this tradition comes from the early works of Pagan author Raven Grimassi, although the work of Charles Godfrey Leland (specifically *Aradia, or the Gospel of the Witches*) is a source of inspiration for some Strega.

There are strong similarities between Stregheria and Wicca: They both honor a single God and Goddess; hold eight annual holy days; and have closed groups and ritual nudity as part of their practice. Another strong similarity includes claims of being an ancient religion. As with Wicca, there is a distinct lack of evidence to support this, such as that the word "stregheria" itself is not common in the Italian language (*streghnoria* is the common word for witchcraft and carries negative connotations).

Stregheria is sometimes called *La Vecchia Religione* ("the old religion") or the Elder Faith.

Wicca

Although Wicca originated as a coven-based initiatory mystery religion, it has evolved into a largely solitary-practiced religion with a strong focus on nature, the seasonal cycle, and finding balance. Many traditions exist within Wicca, with some tracing their lineage back to Gerald Gardner, the founder of Wicca, through diligent adherence to rites, deities honored, and training material. These traditions are frequently distinguished by being called British Traditional Wicca (BTW).

Generally, Wicca is practiced much more loosely than within BTW. Members freely find inspiration in other religions and spiritual practices, blending them with the ritual format, pair of complementary deities, and religious calendar of Wicca to create something unique to them. Wicca is strongly focused on the sacredness of nature and believes in the necessity for people to find balance in their lives and with nature. Common spiritual practices include magick (as Wicca is a form of religious witchcraft), divination, healing, spiritism, and rituals aligned to the lunar and seasonal cycles.

Witchcraft

Less a tradition and more a spiritual practice, witchcraft is inherently secular yet prominent within Paganism. It is frequently practiced in conjunction with other traditions or as part of the foundation of those traditions. For example, Wicca is a form of religious witchcraft: All Wiccans are witches, yet not all witches are Wiccan. There are numerous religious witchcraft traditions, such as Feri Witchcraft, Reclaiming Tradition, and the Clan of Tubal Cain.

Distinguishing witchcraft from other systems of magick is a strong focus on the physical world and everyday life. The goal of the witch is not to escape life, to attain godhead, or to transcend the physical world. Impressing the importance of physicality on us while simultaneously encouraging efficacy in wielding spiritual forces. The magick typically focuses on creating change in our everyday lives, such as casting spells to be more successful in our careers or creating charms to protect our homes and families.

Engaging with spirits through a relationship-based approach is also a defining trait of witchcraft. These spirits may originate within the land, such as spirits of place or the spirits within plants, stones, and rivers, or they may exist solely within the spirit world. Witchcraft is founded on animism—the belief that the world is alive with spirits—and emphasizes personal responsibility, accountability, and empowerment. Witchcraft can be practiced within or without any religious context, yet many witches find the Pagan community to be more accepting of their practice than mainstream religions.

Diversity and Inclusion

There are few generalizations that can be made about the individuals who make up the Pagan community. Despite a general focus on ancient European religions, Pagans are found throughout the world and come from varied cultural backgrounds. However, the greatest numbers of Pagans tend to live within the United States, the United Kingdom, Canada, and Australia, with increasing numbers of Pagans found in South America and Brazil.

Paganism is open to individuals of all races, and many Pagans take a firm stance against white supremacy and racial discrimination in their traditions. These efforts can be seen in the strongly worded mission statements of Pagan organizations, the removal of individuals from leadership positions after being found to promote such ideologies, and active work within prisons to ensure incarcerated Pagans receive equal religious rights but also to prevent the co-option of Paganism by racist and white-supremacist groups. In this way, the Pagan community embodies its shared values and commitment to diversity by working to hold each other accountable.

Paganism is generally sex-positive and embraces LGBTQIA+ individuals, celebrating differences as a source of strength within our communities. Men, women, trans men, trans women, and nonbinary individuals are all welcome under the Pagan umbrella. Leadership positions in most traditions are open to LGBTQIA+ individuals, and there are even Pagan traditions that focus exclusively on LGBTQIA+ individuals and their unique experiences. This inclusive attitude and celebration of differences is part of why so many people feel as if they've "come home" when discovering Paganism.

Pagans can be found in major metropolitan areas as much as in suburbs and rural areas. Although our traditions are Earth-based, we recognize that just because there exists a city atop it, the land hasn't gone away. There are land spirits everywhere, and there are some spirits who are unique to cities. Cities and rural areas alike hold lessons for us and opportunities to connect with the land and the Gods in different ways. Many deities even have traditional associations with cities, which allows a unique opportunity to connect with Them that cannot be experienced in a rural setting.

There are no socioeconomic standards, as Pagans come from all walks of life and hold all manner of careers. Teachers, doctors, writers, artists, politicians, police officers, soldiers, professional witches, psychics, athletes, musicians . . . if you can think of it, there's a good chance that more than a few Pagans hold that job as a means of supporting themselves and see no conflict between their work and their religious beliefs.

While formal education varies, most Pagans consider research and study to be an important part of their practice. Most people find their way to Paganism from other religions and practice as solitaries, so an affinity for reading is essential to develop a strong foundation for their spiritual practice and strong relationships with the Gods. As time passes, more individuals are being born into Paganism, and there are now some people who can lay claim to being a third-generation Pagan.

Looking at
Population Statistics

Although exact numbers are impossible to calculate, in 2014 the Pew Research Center published a report that estimated about 1.5 million Americans identify as Wiccan or Pagan. This number isn't entirely accurate, as many Pagans may have chosen "nonreligious" or "other" due to the private nature of their beliefs and practices. There were also likely a number of Pagans who did not participate in the survey at all. However, this number does show a significant increase in the US Pagan population compared to Trinity College's earlier studies, which reported 8,000 Wiccans in 1990 and a significantly larger estimate of 340,000 in 2008 (the last time they conducted such research).

Due to some of the inherent problems with these surveys (such as Christian bias in questioning and that outside research has found that a significant number of non-Christian individuals do not respond truthfully to survey questions), the researchers at ReligiousTolerance.org have taken this same data, along with conservative growth estimates and additional data (such as increase in Pagan book titles and sales) and reached different conclusions. They estimated 2 million Wiccans in the US in 2015, and 3 million in 2018. They do not have estimates for Pagans as a whole. Even if we only accept the more conservative estimate from the Pew Research Center, an estimate of 1.5 million puts Paganism as the third-largest religion in the US. (Note that Christianity is the largest with 70.6 million, and Judaism the second largest with 1.9 million.)

In the United Kingdom, the 2011 UK census reported 53,172 individuals identified as Pagan in England and Wales alone, while 11,026 identified as Wiccan, and another 3,946 identified as Druid. Combining these numbers with the number of people who identified as Pantheist, Heathen, Witch, Shaman, Animist, Occultist, Reconstructionist, and Thelemite, there are 75,281 self-identified people who would fall under the Pagan umbrella.

Scholars within the Pagan community have estimated this number to be considerably higher, looking at membership for large organizations among other factors. However, the obstacles to a more accurate estimate are the same in the UK as in the US.

It's worth taking into consideration the work of Helen A. Berger, who conducted two surveys 15 years apart (the Pagan Census, which was based solely in the US, and the Pagan Census Revisited, which was international). Although not true censuses, her work shows a significant increase in solitary practitioners (consisting of 51 percent in the Pagan Census and 79 percent in the Pagan Census Revisited), with just 36 percent of Pagans surveyed stating that they have received training within a group. Her findings also demonstrate the significant growth the Pagan population continues to experience.

CHAPTER 3
Pagan Deities

Perception of the Divine and how we are meant to interact with it are two of the hallmarks of any religion. The worldview and deities acknowledged within Paganism may not be unique to this religious movement, but they encourage the diversity the Pagan community is known for while also instilling the sense of kinship necessary for any community to flourish. In this chapter, we'll look closely at the diverse Pagan perceptions of deities.

Deities

A central component of Paganism is the belief in—and worship of—deities. A deity is a spiritual being, lacking physical form and comprised of energy alone, who is able to exert significant power within the physical world and the spirit world alike. As energetic beings, deities fall onto a spectrum of spirits, distinguished by Their power and level of awareness. Whether a God or Goddess is a deity through nature or through an assumed role is a matter of speculation with no hard opinions one way or another in Paganism.

Although most Pagans are polytheists (honoring multiple deities), the word "deity" will often be used in a catch-all manner. For example, when dealing with a challenging life situation, it wouldn't be unusual for one Pagan to ask another, "Have you asked Deity?" This deliberately vague usage acknowledges that:

Pagans worship a variety of gods and goddesses;

the individual may have a relationship with many deities, but there is one who is best consulted on this matter;

not all Pagans feel comfortable identifying the deities they honor to others;

not all Pagans are comfortable saying the name of *any* deity aloud.

Forging and maintaining strong relationships with deities forms the basis of spiritual practice for many Pagans. What that looks like will vary from person to person, though, as no two Pagans will have the same practice, even if they belong to the same tradition and worship the same deities. Remember, your personal practice is *personal*. What you need out of a spiritual practice will differ from what I need out of a spiritual practice, and that's exactly how it's meant to be in Paganism.

In desiring a relationship with the Gods, knowing whom you should approach first can feel daunting. There are many different pantheons and deities to choose from. How do you know you're worshiping the *right* deity for you?

When it comes to the Gods, there is no *right* or *wrong* deity. They are people, like you and me, with Their own predilections and interests. They don't owe you anything, and They have every right to choose whom They develop close relationships with—just as you have the same right to decide with whom you develop close relationships. Yet most Gods are frequently more willing than not to acknowledge those who enter into relationship with them, and They are also typically very generous with their patience with us. This removes the pressure of worrying about "doing it wrong," as there are no mistakes you can make with the Gods if you approach Them with sincerity and respect.

To begin honoring the Gods, it's acceptable to start by worshiping just a few deities. You are not any more or less Pagan whether you honor one or two deities or you honor a dozen deities. It is better to have strong relationships with a few Gods than to create obligations for yourself that you cannot maintain. Consider the deities to Whom you feel most drawn. Perhaps there are qualities or traits about Them that you admire or that you'd like to more strongly embody. Perhaps there is something in the mythology of that deity that lights a fire within you and fills you with wonder. Or perhaps you already feel a call from a particular deity, with Their name and attributes appearing in unexpected circumstances. These are great ways to initially narrow your options so you can further research and begin honoring these Gods. (At the end of this chapter, page 41, see the list of deities for brief introductions to help you begin your research.)

Once you've established which deities you would like to approach, you'll need to introduce yourself. Remember, the Gods are unique beings. They may choose to bestow blessings on you and aid you in your life, but they aren't *obligated* to do so. Note that it's rude to call the Gods for the very first time and immediately make requests. Enter into the relationship slowly, as you would with a new, respected friend.

To introduce yourself, first ensure that you do so in a place and time when you expect no interruptions. That may mean waiting until your housemates or children are in bed or even waking up a little bit earlier than you normally do in the morning. Next, create a welcoming environment for that deity. You are inviting Them into your home, so be sure to treat Them with hospitality. You needn't erect an elaborate altar or shrine: A clean space atop a table, a single candle, and enough room before it to make an offering is simple, yet sufficient.

Act without expectation of receiving a response. Expectations interfere with remaining spiritually (and psychically) open, as they prime your mind to only recognize responses that fit those parameters. This means that if the deity you're making offerings to responds in a different way than you expect, you likely won't notice.

Light the candle and address that deity. You can recite a poem or hymn to them, consulting ancient sources such as the *Orphic Hymns* of ancient Greece, for example. You can also speak from the heart, allowing whatever words come to flow freely as you call to that deity. Now, give an offering or libation as you introduce yourself. This offering could be a glass of wine or liqueur, honey, fresh fruit, or home-baked goods. Hold the offering in the air before the candle. State your name and why you have called Them. Don't overcomplicate or overthink it. You can say something like "Deity, my name is ___. Please accept this offering and know that I desire to know you better and feel your presence within my life." Then place the offering before the candle.

When you are finished, extinguish the candle but allow the setup and offering to remain for a while. Overnight is ideal; if this is difficult because you don't have a set space to make offerings to the Gods, allow the offering to sit for several minutes before disposing of it. Libations can be poured onto the ground outside, buried, or, if no other options exist, poured down the drain of your kitchen sink. Offerings shouldn't be placed outside unless buried, as they can attract wildlife that may not be able to safely eat the offering. It is fine to place the offerings into the compost (or trash if no other options exist).

Repeat this simple ritual, lighting a candle and giving an offering or libation without expectation, again in a few days. In this way, you will show the Gods that you are sincerely interested in Them, and you are more likely to receive a response that your offerings are welcome.

Don't despair if there is no noticeable response to your efforts. The Gods don't always respond, and when They do, it's often subtle and easy to miss until you sharpen your intuition and spiritual skills. You can facilitate the strengthening of these skills by learning to remain open and aware, strengthening your intuition, and regularly practicing divination (asking whether your offering was well received is a great focus for your readings as you learn and practice).

Know that it is okay to begin honoring one deity only to later feel drawn to more intensely worship another deity. Your spiritual journey is not static; it will change as you change. As you grow and meet your spiritual needs, you'll discover new needs. This naturally means that some deities will be more prominent in your life during certain times and not at all during others, and that is perfectly normal.

Monotheism

When we think about religion in general terms, typically a monotheistic religion comes to mind. Yet in the broad scope of the world's history, monotheism is relatively new and unusual in that most of the world's religions have been polytheistic or animistic. This stands in stark contrast to the dominating presence that monotheism currently has, as seen in the prevalence of Christianity, Judaism, and Islam, which are also referred to as the Abrahamic religions, as they share early prophets and originated within the same area of the world (the Middle East).

Monotheism is the religious view that there is one deity alone who exists. Monotheistic religions frequently embrace dualism as a world view, the belief that there is a separation between humans and the Divine, extending to a separation between humans and the spirit world or afterlife. This necessitates the need for religious specialists to intervene on behalf of the people to communicate with their deity so that proper modes of interacting with that deity, such as rituals and worship, can be known and adhered to. These religious specialists may take the form of ordained clergy as well as prophets. Members of monotheistic religions are also sometimes called "people of the book," as these religions possess sacred texts detailing their philosophy, mythology, and legends.

Pagan traditions tend to be polytheistic or pantheistic, yet some monotheistic Pagans can be found, such as those who follow the Dianic Wiccan tradition and some practitioners of ceremonial magic. However, no Pagan tradition possesses a sacred text or strict dogma detailing "proper" belief or practice. Paganism also isn't conducive to the presence of prophets due to a lack of dualism and to the fact that many traditions encourage members to develop skills in divination and spiritism, allowing members to approach the Gods on their own.

Polytheism

Polytheism is the belief in—and acknowledgment of—a multitude of individual and autonomous deities. These deities can take many forms, including masculine, feminine, androgynous, intersex, and even zoomorphic (appearing as animals or bearing animal features and characteristics). These deities are typically tied to the physical world in some way, being viewed as the movers and shakers within the world. As such, many deities are connected to natural phenomena and features, such as weather patterns, forests, and mountains, as well as various stages of life, such as childhood, pregnancy, marriage, and death. These deities are typically viewed as having complex relationships with each other, often marrying and producing children as well as warring and holding grudges against each other. In this way, deities within a polytheistic worldview frequently exhibit what we would consider to be human emotional qualities, yet this familiarity in behavior shouldn't be taken as cause to underestimate the power They wield.

Most world religions are polytheistic as well as animistic. This worldview believes in the existence of numerous deities, lesser divine beings, and other spirits. This makes polytheists, regardless of originating culture, generally welcoming to other religions and their deities. These outside deities are not generally viewed as a threat but, rather, are seen as heretofore unknown beings of power equally worthy of praise and honor. This is why we can trace the spread and reach of certain deities across a region as They were welcomed and adopted by new cultures that came into contact with that deity.

Most Pagan traditions tend to be polytheistic or pantheistic. While a polytheist believes in distinct and knowable deities Whom we can approach and speak with, and Who will grant us Their favor, a pantheist does not believe in distinct deities, seeing the Divine present in all things.

This worldview rejects the idea of knowable deities and holds the Divine to be impersonal. Pantheists frequently work with deities in the form of archetypes, as symbolic patterns of energy represented by the dominant traits assigned to a deity. For example, as an archetype, the Greek goddess Artemis may be viewed as a huntress and provider or as a protector of women and children. Note that polytheists do not work with archetypes but with unique deities who are viewed as people. The Gods are not viewed as correspondences—means of adding additional or specific types of energy to magick or ritual—but as beings we strive to honor through devotion and the heart-felt development of personal relationships with Them.

Animism

This is the belief that all things contain an animating spirit—not just living beings, but inanimate objects, such as rocks, mountains, rivers, and storms, as well as man-made objects. The animist worldview stands in contrast to the general attitude within Western society that sees the natural world as a resource and man-made objects as generally disposable. Animism is a worldview that has a beautiful quality of drawing you outside of yourself and encouraging you to be more aware of—and responsive to—your surroundings. It places you more fully into the natural world, not outside of it or lording over it as a "steward." Instead, animism posits you as but one of many beings who share this world and asks that you consider your relationships with these spirit beings.

When you see the world as alive with spirits, it requires you to change your behavior and acknowledge the ways that your behavior hurts the other-than-human beings who share the land with you. It forces you to have a more invested interest in your local areas, in the land beneath your feet, rather than focusing on nature as a romantic concept or as only being found in pristine wilderness.

Many Pagans subscribe to an animist worldview to some degree. Some traditions and practices, such as Druidry and witchcraft, have animism as a defining trait. Although animism is not a religion, it is the oldest worldview on our planet and continues to be a dominating worldview, often going hand in hand with polytheism. Animism is a holistic outlook that emphasizes the importance of your physical body and your spirit body, that both are important and necessary for healthy living, and that the physical world and the spirit world overlap.

Mythology

Religion is, at the most basic level, a means of understanding the world in which we live. Mythology is the collection of stories we tell regarding religion, particularly in regard to the big questions that religion strives to answer. Myths encompass cosmology (how the world came to be) as well as eschatology (how the world will end, if ever). They tell us how the Gods came to be and the trials and victories They faced. Myths tell us how humans came to be, tell us why we came to be, and explain our relationship to the Gods.

Although some religions understand their mythology from a literal standpoint, Paganism tends to view mythology as layered stories. Understanding and more fully appreciating a myth requires you to consider those layers individually and collectively. This approach presents you with deeper meaning that can provide you a more complete picture of the Gods, clarify your place in the world, and reveal clues to those big questions we all grapple with as part of being alive. In this way, mythology serves not just to inspire but also to comfort, helping us make sense of our existence.

Pagans generally have a love of ancient mythology and find relevance in these stories across time. As Paganism is typically focused on reviving the worship of ancient deities, both by reconstructing ancient worship and by creating new means of worship and ritual, these stories and legends provide a source of inspiration and material to guide our rites. When you are creating new practice around the Gods, mythology provides you with a starting point, showing you things that a certain God may prefer as offerings and libations, for example.

Pantheon

The deities recognized within a religion are often unique to that religion and are collectively called that religion's pantheon. Think of Them as the family of deities and beings of power most strongly associated with that religion or culture. As Paganism is a collection of traditions, there is no Pagan pantheon—but that doesn't stop us from having many gods. Pagans are generally concerned with reviving the religions surrounding ancient deities in some way, so our Gods and Goddesses come from many different pantheons. These pantheons may originate from vastly different peoples and climates, such as the Greeks and Romans of the Mediterranean or the Germanic peoples of Northern Europe. But these pantheons tend to be indigenous to Europe and not possess living traditions—that is, the religions surrounding these deities no longer exist, as they were exterminated by early Christians. After all, you can't revive what already exists.

Knowing from which culture and from where these deities come is important, as these things influence not just the stories surrounding the Gods but also Their personalities and general areas of power. It's also important because not all pantheons and deities are necessarily open to us. Just because a pantheon is ancient does not automatically open it up to modern Pagans—living religions of those deities must be considered. It is disrespectful to choose to honor a deity in your own way or within the context of a Pagan tradition if that deity already has a living and established religion surrounding Them. If you are sincere in your desire to honor a deity, you need to be willing to pursue the living traditions around that deity as those traditions formed around the guidance and preferences of that deity. To ignore these living traditions is to ignore the wishes of that deity, which makes it likely that the deity will ignore your efforts to honor Them. Doing so is also a form of cultural appropriation: It divorces aspects of a culture (in this case, a deity) from the context of that culture while passing off your use of that aspect (in this case, worship of that deity) as equal to that of the original culture.

Discovering Deities

Although it cannot compare to deep study of a deity and ritual action to meet that deity, the following list is intended to help introduce you to some of the Gods and Goddesses Who are prominent within Paganism.

- **Apnu (ancient Egypt):** Apnu was known as Anubis by the Greeks. He is a god of the Underworld and death, charged with watching over the process of preparing a body for entombment, including mummification and embalming. He is depicted as having the head of a jackal.

- **Apollo (ancient Greece):** The twin brother of Artemis, Apollo is a god of music, prophecy, archery, and healing. He is typically associated with the sun and wolves and is a protector of young boys. The Oracle at the Temple of Apollo at Delphi was highly renowned and consulted for prophecy.

- **Artemis (ancient Greece):** The twin sister of Apollo, Artemis is a goddess of hunting, supplying the Gods with game. She is a protector of young girls as well as pregnant and laboring women. She is also associated with dancing and choral music, archery, the moon, and antlered deer.

- **Athena (ancient Greece):** Athena, also called Athene, is the goddess of battle strategy, wisdom, courage, and crafts (especially weaving). She is a clear-sighted goddess who sees much.

- **Bastet (ancient Egypt):** Depicted with the head of a lioness, Bastet is a goddess of the home and domesticity, as well as childbirth, fertility, and sexual pleasure. She is a protector of the home and against disease. She is also known as Bast, Baast, Baset, and Ubasti.

- **Brighid (ancient Ireland):** Also known as Brigit and Brigid (all pronounced "breed"), Brighid is a goddess of inspiration, healing, the hearth fire, metalsmiths, poets, cattle, and the arrival of spring.

- **Ceridwen (ancient Wales):** Ceridwen is a goddess of inspiration, transformation, and rebirth. She possesses a cauldron filled with *awen*, divine inspiration.

- **Cernunnos (ancient Gaul):** A popular Celtic deity, Cernunnos is known primarily from imagery. He is depicted with antlers, sitting cross-legged, wearing a torque, and surrounded by animals, such as an antlered snake.

- **Danu (ancient Ireland):** Danu is the mother of the Tuatha Dé Danann ("people of Danu," a supernatural race of people; this title refers to some of the Irish deities Who, in later stories, become mixed up with the fae). Perhaps the embodiment of the Danube River, She is a goddess of sovereignty, power, waterways, the wind, and the earth.

- **Demeter (ancient Greece):** Demeter was the mother of Kore, who would become Persephone. She is a goddess of agriculture and the fertility of the Earth. She is the driving force behind the seasons, as it is when Her daughter resides in the Underworld for part of the year that Her grief causes nothing to grow.

- **Epona (ancient Gaul):** Epona is a Celtic goddess of horses and fertility, but much of what we know about Her, historically, comes from the Romans. She is associated almost exclusively with the protection of horses.

- **Freyja (ancient Scandinavia):** Associated with love, beauty, and seiðr (a distinctly Heathen form of magick), as well as war and death, Freyja is a goddess who struck a deal with Odin and holds claim to half of all who are struck down in battle. She rides in a chariot pulled by two cats.

- **Hekate (ancient Greece):** A complex goddess of considerable power, Hekate is now most widely known for Her associations with crossroads, the night, witchcraft, the dead, and necromancy. Yet Her power is so vast that She was frequently conflated with other goddesses, such as Artemis and Demeter, among others.

- **Hel (ancient Scandinavia):** A fearsome goddess, Hel ruled over a part of the Underworld where those who died a dishonorable death, of old age, or of illness were sent. She is depicted as being half living flesh and half rotting.

- **Hera (ancient Greece):** Wife of Zeus, king of the Gods, Hera is a goddess of marriage, women, childbirth, and family. She is a powerful goddess who has control of the skies. Peacocks are sacred to Her.

- **Hermes (ancient Greece):** Hermes is a god of liminality and movement, serving as a messenger for the Gods (and therefore associated with communication and travel). He is also cunning and viewed as a trickster god.

- **Horus (ancient Egypt):** Depicted with the head of a falcon, Horus was one of the most important deities of ancient Egypt, serving as protector of the land. He is associated with the rulership of kings as well as the skies.

- **Isis (ancient Egypt):** One of the most prominent deities, Isis was the wife of Osiris, a goddess of life, magic, and wisdom, and a protector of women and children. She is frequently depicted with the wings of kites or falcons.

- **Loki (ancient Scandinavia):** A god of cunning and trickery, Loki is able to change His physical form and sex, which leads Him to be both father and mother to a number of other deities. He is generally unconcerned for the well-being of others as well as societal standards.

- **Lugh (ancient Ireland):** Lending His name to the festival Lughnasadh, Lugh is associated with the rulership of kings, oaths, and skill. He is a warrior and master craftsman.

- **The Mórrígan (ancient Ireland):** A fearsome goddess of war, prophecy, and death, the Mórrígan is sometimes seen as a triple goddess, though there are variations concerning which three goddesses together form Her. A shapeshifter, She frequently takes the form of a raven, a young maiden, a queen ready for battle, and a wizened elderly woman.

- **Odin (ancient Scandinavia):** Odin is the chief of the Norse gods and associated with wisdom, battle, divination (for He is the one Who discovered the runes), and magic. He is a complex and cunning god.

- **Osiris (ancient Egypt):** Ruling over the Underworld, Osiris is a god of fertility, death, mummification, and resurrection. He is depicted with green skin and mummy-wrapped legs.

- **Set (ancient Egypt):** Associated with war and chaos, Set is a violent god of storms, trickery, and the desert who provided balance within the Egyptian pantheon.

- **Skaði (ancient Scandinavia):** Skaði is a goddess of hunting, depicted carrying a bow and wearing snowshoes or skis. Although She lives in the mountaintops where the snow never melts, She is far more benevolent than other Norse figures, such as the giants, who also were associated with snow, cold, and ice.

- **Thor (ancient Scandinavia):** Depicted carrying a large hammer called Mjölnir, Thor is associated with thunder, lightning, and strength. He is the protector of humans and is frequently depicted as having a short temper, red hair, and a red beard.

- **Tyr (ancient Scandinavia):** Tyr is an upholder of law and justice, as well as a principal war deity alongside Odin and Thor, able to incite strife. The most notable story about Him tells of the sacrifice of His arm in order to bind the wolf-god, Fenrir, Whom the other gods feared.

- **Zeus (ancient Greece):** The king of the Greek Gods, Zeus is associated with strength and power, ruling over the skies and maintaining order among the Gods and humankind. He is father to many gods, mortals, and divine beings, with His sexual exploits being prominent in His mythology.

Satan: A Social Misconception

◇◇

A popular misconception about Paganism is that it is "devil worship"—idolizing Satan, a Christian concept. Rather, as much as Paganism is polytheistic and welcoming to deities of other religions, Christianity is a living religion that has had a historically hostile relationship with both modern Paganism and ancient Paganism. This causes Pagans to generally stay away from Christian concepts, mythology, and beings of power. You won't find Pagan rituals calling on Satan, just as you won't find Pagans calling the Christian God into their rites. These beings are simply outside the scope of Paganism and aren't compatible with the Pagan worldview.

The monotheistic worldview of Christianity is incompatible with the polytheistic worldview of Paganism, contributing to a clear separation between Christian and Pagan practices. Paganism doesn't have any cut-and-dry concepts of good and evil, recognizing that as nature is both creative and destructive, ordered and chaotic, each person holds the potential to do great good as well as great harm. Pagans see this as a matter of personal choice, not inherent quality, and the consequences of those actions may be played out in this lifetime and/or in a future incarnation.

That many Pagans believe in reincarnation (or the idea that we will experience many lifetimes) also precludes the inclusion of Satan in Pagan practices: That we will be born, live, and die only to be reborn again and again is incompatible with the existence of an evil being bent on tempting us to sin so we spend the afterlife in punishment. While Satan may be an important and useful concept within Christianity, he remains incompatible with Pagan perceptions of the nature of the self and the afterlife.

CHAPTER 4
Pagan Beliefs

One of the defining traits of any religion is how it views the self and the obligations it imposes on its members through belief. In this chapter, we'll explore the multidimensional view of the self that is prominent within Paganism and look at some of the more common values.

A Vast Belief System

There can be a lot of variation among Pagans in terms of belief systems. After all, we are a diverse community that celebrates our differences and actively strives to maintain that diversity. We encourage each other to trust our intuition, listen to the Gods, and follow the path to which we feel called. But there are a few common beliefs that can be found across traditions and individual practitioners. These beliefs are generally Earth-based (rooted in the reality that the Earth is sacred and central to spiritual practice) and polytheistic (founded on the existence of numerous individual and unique deities).

Right of choice. Pagans believe that you have the right to decide what you believe in, what religions you subscribe to, and how involved you want to be. That means that if you feel called to pursue the priesthood of a particular deity, you'll find support and guidance within the community to do so. But if you feel that quietly honoring the Wheel of the Year and actively making environmentally friendly changes to your lifestyle is as satisfying and deep as you need to go, you'll find that your choice is also celebrated and supported.

Personal responsibility. Rather than a universal code of ethics, within Paganism, personal responsibility is stressed. This means you are not just accountable for the consequences of your actions, but you are responsible for your spiritual practice, for ensuring that your practice is meeting your spiritual needs, and for staying focused on your personal and spiritual growth. There is no threat of punishment or reprisal; there's no spiritual being watching you to make sure you behave; there is only you, doing the work to hold yourself accountable and to live with integrity.

An open-minded approach to deities. While generally polytheistic, Paganism encourages us to freely choose how we view the Divine and the level of interaction we desire. We are free to approach the Gods as we will, building relationships with those deities we feel drawn to or Who make Themselves known to us and call us to Their worship. We may worship Them with varying degrees of intensity and regularity, as we determine and as They require of us. There are no ideal standards, just the encouragement to form those relationships and to let those relationships change us for the better.

Universal consciousness. Humans are not unique in possessing consciousness and are not seen as superior to other beings with whom we share the Earth—that includes plants and trees, rivers and lakes, mountains and hills, and the very real noncorporeal beings we call spirits and deities. The reality of a world thrumming and alive with spirits means that we stand in a place of equality with other beings: not exalted and not in a position as saviors or heroes, but on equal ground where our differences are viewed without value-based judgments assigned to them. We are one type of being in a universe filled with so many different ways to be, and each of these beings—no matter how different from us—is filled with meaning and worth.

Inherent sacredness. The physical world and physicality are a unique way of being that doesn't happen by accident. There is meaning and importance to this, a quality of sacredness and divine inspiration that warrants reverence and celebration. It is a joy to be alive, to be physically incarnate, to experience the wonders of this world that we can only know because of our physical bodies. We don't scorn the flesh in favor of the spirit but view both as essential and necessary, both as a blessing and imbued with the sacred.

Connection with the universe. There exists among all things a connection. This connection is energetic and, thus, allows the free flow of information along these lines of connection. Through these connections, you are able to gauge the energetic currents active in your life, gaining insight into situations and decisions you're making, and even to receive messages from the Gods and your ancestors. These connections also allow signs and synchronicities to reach you. These are energetic sign-posts that carry meaning for good and bad, demanding your attention and reminding you to stay engaged.

Consciousness beyond death. We are both body and spirit for a reason. While the body is temporary, the spirit is eternal and carries with it a bit of your personality that lasts after death. This allows you to communicate with the dead (such as your ancestors), to receive guidance and maintain strong relationships. Many Pagans believe in reincarnation, that the spirit will experience physicality again and again, with your spirit incarnating into a new body after a period of rest in which you integrate the lessons learned in life and recover from the stress of living.

Accepting Other Beliefs

Although many Pagans have strong opinions regarding their beliefs and practices, they generally hold an appreciative view of other religions, recognizing that there is no one religion or form of spiritual practice that is right for everyone. Each of our personal journeys will be different, and we will each be called by different deities and moved by different religious models. That we are able to choose the religion (or lack thereof) to which we subscribe is a privilege that we recognize and celebrate as part of our commitment to individual autonomy.

With this understanding, it's not unusual for someone to be committed to their practice and sincere in their worship yet still be inspired by other religions. In these instances, it can be tempting to adopt the elements of that religion that most appeal to us, but doing so is strongly discouraged, as this is a form of appropriation and spiritual theft. Those religious elements will not have the same impact when stripped of the greater religious context, as it is that context that informs their meaning and that makes them so powerful in the first place. Removing that context erases the deeper meaning of why that element exists within that religion and makes its inclusion within another religious context awkward and without purpose.

Occasionally, Pagans will come across a religion or belief system that doesn't align with ours, in such a way that it's difficult to remain appreciative. Sometimes world-view and values can be so incompatible that there may appear to be little common ground. Open conversation isn't always possible or desired in these instances, so it isn't unusual for Pagans to keep quiet about their beliefs and practices, unless asked, so as to avoid conflict and maintain a respectful environment, such as when working with individuals with strong religious beliefs that run counter and may even be hostile to our own.

An Alternative View of the Self

In Paganism, the view of the self can be quite freeing when compared to views held within dominant Western religions. While the latter frequently view people as inherently flawed and in need of divine intervention to be saved, Pagans hold a holistic view of the self. Commonly, Pagans see people as existing on three levels: the physical self, the mental and emotional self, and the spiritual self. These levels of being are interconnected; what affects one level can and does manifest symptoms in the others.

For example, during a period of spiritual growth, when your spirit body is being stretched and strengthened, it is common to experience emotional lability, to be mentally distracted, and to experience physical symptoms like lethargy and digestive issues. Likewise, when going through mental and/or emotional stress, it can be difficult to muster the energy to engage in spiritual practice, and you may experience headaches. Physical imbalance, such as being sick, can cause you to feel emotionally exhausted, your thoughts fleeting, and your spirit body heavy and unresponsive.

When these three levels of being work in harmony, it contributes to overall health. Efforts to maintain that harmony represent an important component of spiritual practice as part of your effort to be responsible for yourself, your well-being, and your spiritual journey. So, while there can be imbalances that require attending to (such as with medical care, rest, healing rituals, purification, shadow work, or soul retrieval), these are temporary deviations from homeostasis. They don't speak to an underlying and inherent condition of the self. According to Paganism, you are whole, unflawed, and multidimensional.

This view of the self is supported by many facets of the Pagan worldview. For example, the existence of a multitude of spirit beings, able to traverse the divide between the physical world and the spirit world, speaks to the existence of our own spirit bodies. Our ability to communicate with these various spirit beings also supports the existence of our own spirit bodies, as it is through this aspect of ourselves that we interact with and interpret psychic phenomena and energetic stimuli. Belief in the inherent sacredness of the world and the importance of personal responsibility encourages you to appreciate all aspects of yourself, viewing your physical body as beautiful and sacred despite dominant cultural attitudes that may urge you to think otherwise.

The belief that the physical body is sacred encourages you to take care of yourself, attending to your physical health, your mental and emotional health, and your spiritual health with equal importance.

This complex view of the self as multifaceted and both transient and everlasting explains why we are intrinsically capable of approaching the Gods and accessing the wisdom of the universe. Through the sheer nature of your being and the connections you share with all, you have the capability and responsibility to make informed choices for yourself, to be aware of yourself and your actions, and to decide for yourself what is right and wrong. You don't need others to assert their opinions over you, to tell you what you can and cannot do, that some things are arbitrarily okay while others are not. As an independent, powerful, and sacred being in your own right, you make these decisions for yourself, creating a personal code of moral conduct while treating others with respect and affording them the same right to make decisions for themselves.

Free to Choose

Freedom of choice and the right to exercise that choice are ingrained within the fabric of Paganism. They are why no explicit dogma or governing code of conduct exists, as these would only undermine personal choice. In Paganism, you are free to decide for yourself what a good life looks like and to do what you deem necessary or what the situation requires to achieve that life. You can pursue whatever career you feel compelled to hold and love whomever your heart chooses regardless of gender, race, or religious beliefs. You can dress as you see fit, eat the foods you most prefer, and live your life in the manner you choose.

On the surface, this may give the impression that Pagans are self-indulgent and live without morals. This is understandable when the dominant model for morality within the Western world is one founded on extensive restrictions. But these restrictions are dependent upon the view that humans and the world we inhabit are inherently immoral. Those restrictions then serve to hold people to a different standard of behavior, elevating them from corruption.

But if you embrace the idea that humans are not flawed and are instead inherently sacred, viewing morality as achieved via restrictions doesn't make sense, as those restrictions may diminish that sacredness. Instead, allowing freedom and the right to choose honors and affirms that sacredness. Through your commitment to holding yourself responsible for those choices and the consequences of your actions and reactions, you honor the sacredness in others as you trust that they will act in a similar manner and hold themselves accountable for their own choices. It's not a perfect system, but it does much to encourage the ethical treatment of others within our communities. It establishes an air of expectations—especially for our leaders—as it implies that as we hold ourselves accountable, so, too, will others be held accountable for their actions.

Ethical Paganism

With this context in mind, there *are* some general ethical guidelines that can be found among Pagans, guiding behavior that shapes our interactions with each other.

Honesty. Truth is not universal. We each shape our own reality to align with our opinions, experiences, and ideals. But you can do much to present yourself and your truth as openly and honestly as possible. When you give your word, mean it. Hold to your promises. Attend to your obligations. Your word should be as good and binding as a signed contract.

Courage. There is much in this world and in life that is uncertain. You will not always have the answers, and you will rarely feel prepared, but you can still try. You can do what you can in that moment and with what you have available to you. To try in the face of fear and the possibility of failure speaks to your character and strength.

Fidelity. It is been said that the only faith that exists in Paganism is in regard to your ability to be faithful. Loyalty to yourself, the Gods, your family members, and your values is how you maintain the bonds of community and demonstrate the nature of your character.

Discipline. The lack of inherent structure in Paganism requires you to develop the discipline to remain focused on growing, learning, and building strong relationships with the Gods, the land, and your ancestors. It is through consistent effort that you achieve results.

Hospitality. How you treat the beings with whom you share the Earth matters. It isn't enough to acknowledge that the world is alive with spirits: You must act upon that knowledge, treating each other and these spirits with care and respect. Hospitality fosters good relationships and, by keeping the welfare of others at the forefront of your thoughts, encourages you to live your values.

Industriousness. In all things to which you apply yourself, your efforts should demonstrate sincerity and a commitment to seeing things through. When you are faced with obstacles, half-hearted effort cannot compete with earnest and diligent attempts to face the obstacles before you and achieve what you set out to accomplish.

Justice. As much as you hold yourself accountable for your actions and choices, Pagans believe that others should be held accountable for their own. Life may not always be fair, but that does not mean that we can't strive to treat each other—and ourselves—fairly.

Peace. Although we each hold the capacity to do great harm and to do great good, it is your choice and your efforts to not do harm that underscore your desire to live in harmony with others and with the land. Peace is not the absence of conflict but the commitment to not instigate or entertain needless disruption.

Self-reliance. The ability to handle yourself in any given situation is a virtue that benefits you as much as it benefits others. Cultivating self-reliance forces you to be self-aware, taking stock of your strengths, weaknesses, and faults so you can address areas where you are lacking and further focus on your personal and spiritual growth. A self-reliant person is not just better able to help themselves but also more strongly positioned to help others.

Wisdom. The cultivation of wisdom is dependent upon a combination of knowledge and experience. Through your mistakes and successes, you learn and grow, uncovering insights into the everyday and into your spiritual practice that serve to inform future experiences.

Kindness. It is all too easy to be cruel and dismissive. But to see others for who they are, to acknowledge the sacred within them, and to treat them with kindness takes effort. It requires you to slow down, to be aware of your thoughts, and to be disciplined in your efforts to treat others with the respect and compassion they deserve.

Strength. Spiritual practice is not easy. You will be tested, and you will be broken so as to be remade. But in each instance, these trials serve not just to help you grow and be more of what we and the Gods need from us but also as reminders of just how strong you truly are. Strength is your ability to keep going when it would be so much easier to give up or to give in.

Open-mindedness. None of us can ever have all the answers, and we will all too often find that we were quite mistaken about something we felt very strongly about. It behooves you to learn to withhold judgment for a time and to remain open to new information. In this way, you leave yourself open to new discoveries, new friends, and new experiences that can change your life for the better.

The Spiritual Search

Modern Paganism is rooted in questioning. Many of us consider ourselves to be lifelong seekers, committed to always learning, always open to new answers to old questions. Curiosity is an encouraged trait, and some degree of skepticism is desired, as it helps you remain aware and think clearly.

Just because a path is spiritual doesn't mean that common sense gets thrown out the window. It's okay to question your experiences and beliefs. It's okay to find holes in those beliefs and to discard them for new beliefs. None of this makes you a bad Pagan; rather, it demonstrates important Pagan values, such as honesty, being open-minded, and taking accountability for your personal and spiritual growth. This questioning is an important part of that growth.

There will be times when your spiritual practice will not make sense to you. What was once a source of comfort and fulfillment may begin to feel stifling, outdated, and even as if it were created for someone else. In these moments, take stock of your beliefs and experiences, look for the things that no longer fit, and take time to sort through your thoughts and feelings to discover why. This process of questioning and searching helps you see where you've grown. And it refocuses your efforts on areas that help you continue growing. Our spiritual journeys are long and winding paths—it is perfectly reasonable to question where you stand and where you're going.

Paganism and Science

While many religions may dismiss science, Paganism embraces modern science and applauds the improvements it continues to deliver to our lives. As a religious movement comprised of numerous traditions, Paganism has no hard views or accepted myths regarding matters like how the Earth and the universe were created, or why humans exist and what the point of that existence is, so there aren't many opportunities for conflict.

Yet many Pagans embrace the practice of magick, and here lies a distinct opportunity for clashing views. Magick is the action of using spiritual forces to create change. These changes can be within your everyday life, they can be within your mental and emotional spheres, or they can exist entirely on the spiritual plane. There are many systems of magick, such as ceremonial magic and witchcraft, as we discussed in chapter 2.

But science can neither prove nor disprove that magick is real. There simply isn't enough measurable evidence to make a determination one way or the other. There have been very few studies focused on uncovering evidence about magick's effectiveness. The few studies that have been done (such as a recent study measuring the effect of energy healing on cancer cells) don't hold up to peer review due to inherent issues with the way the research was conducted.

CHAPTER 5

The Wheel of the Year

Through shared holidays, Pagans find a stronger sense of community. These holidays are collectively called "the Wheel of the Year" and provide a gentle framework for spiritual experiences throughout the year. In "walking the Wheel"—observing these holidays and witnessing the corresponding seasonal changes in nature—you find a way to feel a stronger connection to the Earth while allowing space for your personal relationships with the Gods to flourish.

The Flow of the Seasons

Although there are few hard standards across all Pagan traditions, the rhythm of natural cycles, such as the seasons and the moon, is frequently the basis for how holy days and celebrations are timed. The flow of the seasons in particular is a strong guide for ritual observances, taking into consideration the way the seasons present themselves in local areas. An example of this can be seen in the shared sacredness that harvest events hold across traditions even as they may occur at very different times of the year. In northern climates, where growing seasons are short, harvest celebrations are a prominent focus in Autumn. In warmer areas, harvest celebrations of the first fruits may be held in Spring, as they were in ancient Greece.

In modern times, this concept of basing religious observances on natural cycles can seem out of place even with Paganism's Earth-centric approach. Few of us live our lives in such a way that our existence is pulled directly from the land. We buy our food from stores and restaurants, and our clothing is often made on the other side of the world by people we will never know. Why not base our religious calendars on the Gods? Why focus so strongly on the natural world?

Even if we did wish to base religious observances solely upon the Gods, there's no way to take the Gods out of the natural world. They are the movers and shakers, the power behind natural forces, and many of Their stories are intimately tied to the land and natural cycles. We see this in deities associated with the moon Whose prime feast days occur at the full moon, dark moon, new moon, or a day during the waxing crescent phase. We see this in deities associated with specific rivers Whose prime feast days coincide with the flooding of that river and the renewed fertility of the surrounding land.

And in that way, both the Gods and this timing by natural cycles help restore a connection that is largely absent from Western society, a connection with the natural world and the energetic forces that affect our lives, regardless of how seemingly divorced from them we have become. You can find further meaning when you look at how these natural cycles play out thematically in your everyday life, showing you how your life and the natural world are both ruled by cycles.

Sabbats or Holy Days

It's this cyclical relationship that is a large part of the modern Pagan concept of the Wheel of the Year. Consisting of eight holy days known as "Sabbats," the Wheel of the Year marks key points of change in the energetic cycles of the natural world as well as rites of passage within the human experience. These Sabbats are then further divided into two groups: Quarter Days and Cross-Quarter Days.

Although most of the Sabbats are inspired by folk and religious holidays of ancient European cultures, there was no single culture that recognized all of these holidays, even by other names. Many of the Sabbats are inspired by the observances of ancient Celtic peoples, although some have no connection to the past outside of a Welsh name. Yet this way of dividing the year into four seasons with a religious observance at the height of each season, as well as at the end of one season and the beginning of another, provides an adaptable structure that encourages diversity of religious expression and spiritual experience.

Note that the Wheel of the Year comes to Paganism from Wicca and is not observed by all Pagan traditions. However, many Pagans do walk the Wheel and use it as the foundation for their ritual celebrations. It is also

WHEEL OF THE YEAR

YULE

DECEMBER 21

SAMHAIN

OCTOBER 31

MABON

SEPTEMBER 21

LUGHNASADH

LITHA

AUGUST 1

WHEEL OF THE YEAR

YULE

FEBRUARY 1

IMBOLC

MARCH 21

OSTARA

MAY 1

BELTANE

LITHA

JUNE 21

Common dates of
observance in the
Northern Hemisphere

The Wheel of the Year   67

common among eclectic Pagans, as it strengthens the sense of community that comes through shared ritual observances—even if those observances happen alone.

Some traditions follow a modified version of the Wheel of the Year with slightly varying foci and different names for the Sabbats, as seen in Druidry and some Heathen groups. Other Pagan traditions have religious calendars that are wholly unique to them, such as Greek Polytheism and Kemeticism. In ancient Greece, many city-states had their own calendars with different names for the months and common feast days. A commonality, however, was that the calendar was based on the solar and lunar cycles combined, known as a "lunisolar" calendar. Modern Greek Polytheists may base their religious calendars on any of the ancient Greek calendars, but the Attic calendar as used in Athens is common. In Kemeticism, timing of holidays varies based upon the geographical location of the Kemetic. For example, a sort of New Year festival known as Wep Ronpet is timed by the heliacal rising of Sirius, which varies based upon latitude. Kemetics may then base timing of other festivals upon this date or follow an established calendar of any groups to which they belong.

Quarter Days

The Quarter Days are solar holidays, taking their timing from key points in the sun's path across the sky in relation to the Earth. Astronomically, these points are known as either solstices or equinoxes. Solstices mark the astronomical time when the sun is at its highest or lowest point in relation to the Earth's equator. These are when we experience the fewest hours of daylight, such as at the Winter Solstice, or the greatest hours of daylight, such as at the Summer Solstice. The equinoxes mark when the center of the sun is directly above the equator, causing there to be roughly equal hours of daylight and darkness. Following the Celtic division of the seasons, each

Quarter Day also marks the midpoint of that season, when its energies are at their peak and strongest. Note that this division does not align with the astronomical division of the seasons and therefore does not match the start of the seasons in our Gregorian calendar or in astrology.

WINTER SOLSTICE

Yule, Midwinter, Alban Arthur

Northern Hemisphere: December 21 to 22; tropical astrology, sun 1° Capricorn
Southern Hemisphere: June 21 to 22; tropical astrology, sun 1° Cancer

Just as the moon waxes and wanes, so does the sun. Since the Summer Solstice, the sun has been waning, the hours of daylight visibly shortening. On the Winter Solstice, the day is at its shortest; this is the longest night, the midpoint of Winter. But, as long and dark as the night may be, we know that the sun will be reborn with the morning, and each day after it will rise a little bit earlier and set a little bit later. Warmth and light will return to the land.

A barren time of rest and reflection, the Winter Solstice is a fire festival, a celebration of family, and a reminder of the cyclical nature of life. Celebration focuses on the lengthening days, the rebirth of the sun, and, of course, feasting with friends and family.

Many common traditions are remarkably similar to, if not the same as, secular Christmas celebrations. Many Pagans will bring boughs of evergreens into their home, a practice rooted in Northern European Midwinter customs, and will also bring in an evergreen tree to decorate, which originated as a Christian practice in Germany. Other traditions include placing a lit candle in every window of the house to encourage the sun to return and "drumming up the sun," in which people stay up until dawn, drumming, in order to awaken the sun.

A barren time of year, the Winter Solstice encourages reflection, asking us to think of those who were there for us during our darkest times, those we are able to count on when things are at their bleakest. We celebrate family, community, and each other to strengthen those bonds and help us get through the remaining weeks of winter.

SPRING EQUINOX

Ostara, Eostre, Vernal Equinox, Alban Eiler

Northern Hemisphere: March 19 to 23; tropical astrology, sun 1° Aries
Southern Hemisphere: September 19 to 23; tropical astrology, sun 1° Libra

Marking the midpoint of Spring, this is a time of transition and change as the days continue to grow longer and warmer. The ice and snow of winter have receded, and green has taken their place, claiming the land and holding it tight in a verdant embrace. The Earth has fully awakened, plants are bursting forth with buds and blossoms, seeds are sprouting and rooting, and animals are active once more.

At the Spring Equinox, day and night are equal in length, with the days getting longer and the nights getting shorter until the Summer Solstice. The focus of celebrations at this time is on the fertility of the land, beginnings, and growth, with eggs, seeds, and flowers being prominent features both symbolically and as components of ritual celebrations.

Common traditions include decorating eggs, such as the Polish *pisanki*, which frequently involves using natural dyes, such as onion skins, turmeric, and beets. These eggs may be used in magick to spread fertility or creative energy, rolled upon the land to transfer the fertility from the egg to the land, or they may be eaten as part of celebrations. If the eggshells are blown out (a method through which the liquid egg is removed and the shell is made hollow) before being dyed, they can be made into fertility charms and keepsake ornaments. Some Pagans will also bless and gift each other seeds, plant seeds for herbs to be used specifically for magick and offerings to the Gods, and go on celebratory walks outside in nature to observe the changes taking place and align themselves with the energy of those changes.

SUMMER SOLSTICE

Midsummer, Litha, Alban Hefin, Alban Heruin

Northern Hemisphere: June 21 to 22; tropical astrology, sun 1° Cancer
Southern Hemisphere: December 21 to 22; tropical astrology, sun 1° Capricorn

The longest day and shortest night, the Summer Solstice marks the peak of the sun's power and strength. As much as that power is lauded and celebrated, we know that tomorrow the sun will begin to wane, the days growing shorter and the nights growing longer until the Winter Solstice. But for today, the land is warm and bright, the sun strong and full of energy.

Embracing and celebrating that power is a prominent focus for this holiday. Bonfires are a central component of many Summer Solstice celebrations, and many Pagans will jump over a bonfire for good fortune and prosperity. Large gatherings are also typical, as the nicer weather makes it easier to come together. Many Druids mark the Summer Solstice with a pilgrimage to Stonehenge to watch the sun rise.

In addition to outdoor festivities and bonfires, common traditions include gathering herbs, as they are believed to possess stronger energy at this time, washing one's face with the morning dew gathered from wildflowers, and performing divination—especially by scrying in the

Midsummer bonfires. Scrying is a divination method that uses a relaxed gaze (directed at fire, smoke, a crystal sphere, a mirror, or water) to allow psychic visions to emerge. This is also a suitable time for magick, as the power of the sun is easily tapped into and directed to create change in your life.

Nature spirits, such as faeries and the land spirits, are believed to be more active at this time of year, and great care is taken to avoid their tricks. Flower chains made of daisies are placed on children to afford them extra protection, and some families may use this as a time to tighten the magickal protection of their home by making new wards (protective charms placed by doors and windows).

AUTUMN EQUINOX

Mabon, Autumnal Equinox, Fall Equinox, Alban Elfed

Northern Hemisphere: September 19 to 23; tropical astrology, sun 1° Libra
Southern Hemisphere: March 19 to 23; tropical astrology, sun 1° Aries

Marking the time when day and night are once again equal in length and power, the Autumn Equinox is a time of abundance and thanksgiving, as it is the second of the three harvest holidays of Autumn (alongside Lammas and Samhain). It is frequently the most labor-intensive of the harvests, as everything ripens at once. Garden fruits and vegetables are brought in by the barrelful, and foraging takes on greater importance as, in many locations, wild herbs are beginning to pull in on themselves, meaning that biennial and perennial plants are pulling nutrients out of aerial parts (leaves and stems) and storing those nutrients in their roots—hence why roots are best gathered in late Autumn. This makes the Autumn Equinox a last chance to gather herbs to keep them well stocked throughout the Winter.

In northern climates, frost can occur at this time, marking the start of the grape and apple harvest. Fittingly, this holiday is sometimes considered a "wine holiday," as wine will be made from the newly harvested grapes and more wine drunk in celebration. The cooler nights mean that this is a time when spiders become more prominent within our homes, taking up residence in quiet corners where they will happily handle troublesome insects.

With a focus on thanksgiving and the abundance of the land, the Autumn Equinox reminds us of the connections we share with others. Few harvests can be completed by one person alone, and this holds true whether we're talking about tomatoes or achieving large goals in our lives. Many Pagans emphasize giving back to the community at this time by giving to charities and food pantries.

Cross-Quarter Days

The Cross-Quarter Days are agricultural holidays, tied to the working of the land and the folk customs surrounding that work, although this is not the full extent of their significance. These holidays are frequently called the Greater Sabbats, as they were the original four holidays of Wicca, from which the Wheel of the Year originated (with the solstices and equinoxes being added later). In keeping with the traditional Celtic division of the seasons, each Cross-Quarter Day marks the beginning of one season and the end of another.

IMBOLC

Imbolg, Candlemas, Brighid's Day, Purification Day, Lady Day, February Eve

Northern Hemisphere: January 31 or February 1 (many American Pagans celebrate February 2 due to Groundhog Day); tropical astrology, sun 15° Aquarius, typically between February 2 and 7

Southern Hemisphere: July 31 or August 1; tropical astrology, sun 15° Leo, typically between August 2 and 7

With the sun reborn at the Winter Solstice, the days have gradually begun to grow longer. Now, the land begins to stir, slowly awakening, and Winter's grip slips from the land. The ice breaks and begins to melt; Spring has come. Although some areas will see Winter attempt to hang on dearly, in others, the ice and snow will continue to melt, and animals, such as sheep, have begun to give birth and now provide milk in a time when family food stores would be growing slim.

In some Pagan traditions, this day is sacred to Brighid, an Irish goddess connected to the hearth and crafting. Many Pagans will make a small doll to represent Her and place it on their shrines or altars. This doll will stay in the house throughout the year to bring blessings and will be replaced at the following Imbolc.

Another common tradition is to bring snow indoors during ritual celebrations, placing it in a bowl or cauldron, so that it melts throughout the ritual, mirroring the melting of the snow and ice outdoors with the gently warming days. Spring cleaning, involving both a deep physical cleaning and a spiritual purification of the home, is also quite common.

BELTAIN

May Day, May Eve, Beltane, Walpurgisnacht

Northern Hemisphere: April 31 or May 1; tropical astrology, sun 15° Taurus, typically between May 2 and 7
Southern Hemisphere: October 31 or November 1; tropical astrology, sun 15° Scorpio, typically between November 2 and 7

Green has fully claimed the land, and everywhere we look we see life and vitality, strength and beauty. The days continue to grow longer, the sun rising just that little bit earlier and setting just that little bit later each day. While the focus of the colder months brings introspection and directs our thoughts toward a focus on spiritual matters, at Beltain, the vibrancy of the Earth bids us to focus on the joy of being alive, the gift of being physically incarnate, and the unique experiences that we are able to have and grow from as a result.

One of the most prominent traditions for Beltain is the European folk custom of dancing around the maypole. Although the original meaning behind the maypole is debated by folklorists, the tall pole—which dancers wind with ribbons as they dance around it—is now frequently viewed as symbolic of heterosexual intercourse between a cis man and cis woman. Yet this speaks more to recent past trends in Paganism, which took the stance of assigning meaning to its customs and even ritual tools based on genitalia and procreation. There is strong evidence that the maypole was merely a highly visible means of showing that warmth and life had returned to the land; the dancing and the decoration of the pole with ribbons and flower garlands were simply a celebration of this.

Some solitary Pagans will create a May Gad, a smaller version of a maypole that can be set upon an altar as the focal point of a solitary Beltain ritual. May baskets are also common. These are small baskets made by weaving strips of paper together. They are then filled with wildflowers and hung from the door of a neighbor—but you must drop off the basket, knock on the door, and leave without letting them know it was you.

LAMMAS

Lughnasadh, August Eve

Northern Hemisphere: July 31 or August 1; tropical astrology, sun 15° Leo, typically between August 2 and 7

Southern Hemisphere: January 31 or February 1; tropical astrology, sun 15° Aquarius, typically between February 2 and 7

With the sun now waning, the days grow shorter but are still warm. The sun's strength and power lessen yet are still unmistakable. This is the first of three harvest holidays that will dominate the Autumn, each with a different focus that draws our attention from the physical world, where it's been all Summer long, and toward the spirit world, where it will remain throughout the Winter season.

At Lammas, the first of the grains are harvested. This also includes the hay harvest, which ensures livestock will be taken care of through the coming Winter. A dominant focus for Lammas is putting those grains to use, particularly in baked goods and bread, making it very much a Sabbat of the home and hearth. Baking bread, even if only to give it as an offering to the Gods or local land spirits, is a common way to celebrate Lammas. Many Pagans will shape their bread, perhaps into the shape of a man to represent various masculine deities. Others may bake traditional European bread recipes, especially those that may be part of their family heritage.

Some Pagan traditions see this day as sacred to the Irish god Lugh, honoring Him through mock battles and the creation of crafts and artwork, as Lugh is both a warrior and a master craftsman.

SAMHAIN

Samhuinn, November Eve

Northern Hemisphere: October 31 or November 1; tropical astrology, sun 15° Scorpio, typically between November 2 and 7
Southern Hemisphere: April 31 or May 1; tropical astrology, sun 15° Taurus, typically between May 2 and 7

The last of the harvest holidays, Samhain marks the harvest of hardy squash, the last of the corn, and root vegetables. The days are dramatically shorter now, and evenings are spent inside to escape the growing cold. After this night, nothing more will be gathered from the fields and gardens; the remaining crops are seen as belonging to the land, and taking them would risk insulting local spirits.

Although the concept of the "thinning veil" is rooted in the Spiritualist movement of the late 1800s and early 1900s, many Pagans hold this night to be a time of increased spirit activity—particularly by the dead—although faeries and land spirits are more apt to be encountered as well. This focus on spirits and our spiritual lives becomes a dominant focus now that will last throughout Winter.

The bulk of Pagan celebrations for Samhain are centered upon the ancestors, both the beloved dead (those who are our ancestors through the bonds of family) and the mighty dead (those who are our ancestors through the bonds of religious community). Shrines are created for the ancestors and decorated with photos, mementos, and candles, as well as libations of water and alcohol and offerings of various foods, especially any favorite dishes of departed family members.

Divination is common on this night, especially with a focus on communicating with your ancestors. Some traditions consider this the start of the New Year and so will divine guidance for the coming year.

Keeping the Wheel of the Year in Perspective

The Wheel of the Year is framed from a perspective taken by ancient Celtic peoples, where both the day and the year are born of darkness. Whereas we commonly view night to be the end of the day, Celtic peoples saw it as the beginning, and so sundown was viewed as the start of a new day. The year was viewed similarly, with Winter not marking the end of the year but, rather, the beginning.

This is why the Cross-Quarter Days are noted as occurring on either the last day of the month or the first day of the next month, as from the Celtic perspective, that Sabbat would begin at sundown of the last day of the month and last until sundown of the first day of the month. For example, Samhain would begin at sundown October 31 and last until sundown November 1. And as Samhain is the first Sabbat of Winter, this is why it marks the beginning of the new year.

It's also important to note that as the Wheel of the Year is based on Celtic celebrations (which have become the Cross-Quarter Days), the seasonal and weather associations typically attributed to them will not hold true in all areas. This is why the Sabbats occur on different dates in the Southern Hemisphere, aligning with the seasons and not the calendar. And this is why many Pagans create new traditions for the Sabbats that are based upon customs and the unique way the seasons unfold where they live.

It is far more important that the way you celebrate the Wheel of the Year helps you connect more deeply with the land where you live than it is to diligently stick to calendar dates and common traditions. So if that means that Lammas is a celebration of the chile harvest for southwest Pagans and that Imbolc is a celebration of the coming ice storm that always happens in mid-February in the northern Midwest, then may your practice be all the better for it, and your connections to the land and the Gods all the stronger.

CHAPTER 6
Rites of Passage

As the Wheel of the Year is a way of following and acknowledging the cycles of the natural world, it also correlates to the cycles that many of us experience throughout our lives. In this way, rites of passage that celebrate these cycles are sometimes viewed as relating to particular Sabbats and seasons due to similarities in theme and energy. Let's explore these associations and a few examples of general rites of passage that are found within Paganism.

Personal Seasons

Just as the natural world is ruled by cycles, so, too, are our lives. We outgrow situations and undergo new experiences that alter how we see the world. We face challenges and emerge changed, with a deeper understanding of ourselves and the world around us. These events and situations come and go, mirroring the path of the sun and moon across the sky, the life cycles of deciduous trees, and the greater birth-life-death-rebirth pattern of our lives.

As the Wheel of the Year marks key points within the flow of the seasons, it also marks the flow of personal seasons in our lives. These personal seasons are acknowledged through rites of passage, a concept found in all cultures throughout the world. These rites signify the importance of many of these dominant cycles and events common to both the human experience and the Pagan experience.

By observing these rites of passage with ritual and ceremony, you strengthen the bonds of community through shared recognition of the struggles, triumphs, and changes you undergo in facing these cycles and events. Rites of passage are how you know you are with people not just of like mind—but also of like experience.

Within Paganism, no standard rites of passage are observed across traditions. Many traditions will have set means of observing these rites—this is part of what makes them a unique tradition. However, there are a few common rites of passages that can be found among the numerous Pagan traditions. Note that we'll discuss these rites of passages using general names, as some traditions may have unique names for the rites based upon how they are viewed and the rituals through which they are observed.

Even though these rites of passage are generally common throughout Paganism, it's important to keep in mind that these rites are largely *celebratory*. We are acknowledging the experiences the individual has gone through and their journey and celebrating the wisdom gained through it, as well as celebrating their entrance into a new chapter of their life and, perhaps even, a new state of being in their life. In this way, these rites of passage don't compare to, say, the sacramental rites of Catholicism. Not only is the basic worldview fundamentally different, but these rites of passage aren't seen as essential to be Pagan. There's no checklist of rites you must tick off in order to be a "full-fledged" Pagan. Some of you may experience all of the following rites of passage. Many will only experience a few of them. Some of these rites of passage are connected to biological functions, and so not everyone is capable of experiencing all of them. And that's okay. It isn't the rites of passage that are important, but the ways that you grow and change throughout your life. Rites of passage in Paganism are a way to celebrate your personal journey.

Many Pagans who practice eclectically or outside of the context of a tradition will create unique rituals to celebrate these personal seasons on their own. The value that comes in acknowledging rites of passage isn't limited to their observance in a group setting. There is just as much value and importance in observing accomplishments and life-changing events through solitary religious ritual as there is within a group setting. So, if you feel the need to ritually celebrate an achievement, a huge decision, or the beginning of a new chapter in your life as a solitary Pagan, do so and know that you have the full support of the Pagan community.

Pregnancy

The arrival of a new baby is an experience that changes the parent's or parents' lives forever. This holds true whether the parent(s) is/are carrying and giving birth to the baby themselves, including a surrogate in the process, or adopting. Pregnancy rites of passage can be modified to the unique circumstances of any family—whether that family begins with a single parent, a couple (married or not), or a polyamorous family, and regardless of whether the parent(s) is/are straight, queer, cis, trans, or nonbinary.

As part of celebrating this experience, pregnancy rites of passage focus exclusively on the parent(s), not the baby. Gifts are typically given that help the parent(s) through this transition, that may help them in caring for their new child, or that are commemorative of this experience. A blessing may be called onto the parent(s) from the Gods. This can be done by a member of the community or by the parent(s) themselves; it doesn't have to be done by Pagan clergy but can be if so desired. If (one of) the parent(s) is pregnant, that blessing may include their belly being anointed with oil or a laying on of hands—but only if that parent is comfortable with this. Some traditions will also include brushing and braiding (if possible) the pregnant parent's hair and generally physically caring for and pampering them.

Although pregnancy rites of passage are held year-round as the need for them arises, they are frequently associated with Summer Solstice, as this is a time when the bounty of the land is not yet ready to be harvested but there is such growing promise.

Baby Welcomings

Celebrations to welcome a new baby are held for babies born into established families, to new parents, or to a new parent, as well as for families who adopt children.

The emphasis isn't so much on this rite of passage being for a baby as it is on welcoming a new young person into that family and, more importantly, into the larger community.

Baby welcoming ceremonies are not comparable to Christian baptisms or christenings, as the only promises made are by the community to the child. There is no obligation for the child or anything expected of them as a result of participating in a Pagan baby welcoming ceremony. This is also not a ceremony that makes the child a Pagan by association or by a metaphysical action that alters them on a spiritual level. While many Pagans do raise their children within their religion, ultimately, we are each responsible for our religious choices and are free to determine our level of involvement—this includes children.

The promises made by the community to the child are typically along the lines of promising to help watch out for them, to protect and guide them in life, to offer friendship, and to be an example of right behavior. Sometimes, these promises can include teaching them Pagan religious ways, answering questions honestly if ever the child needs answers, and helping them know the Gods. In this way, the community pledges a joint responsibility to the child that also serves to affirm the bonds of community.

Blessings may also be called for the child, but again these do not impart any obligation unto the child. It is merely a means of asking the Gods to protect the child. Sometimes a baby welcoming or blessing ceremony will also include naming the child. In this way, the ceremony is a way of presenting the new child to the community, introducing them, and welcoming them into the community.

While baby welcoming ceremonies are held as they are needed (typically soon after the birth or adoption), they are associated with the Spring Equinox, a time when it is common to see young animals and new plant growth in nature.

Handfasting and Marriage

The Pagan community is unique in that it recognizes a union between individuals as valid whether that union is recognized legally or by the community alone. It also recognizes unions existing not just between two people but also among multiple individuals in polyamorous relationships. These unions are viewed as valid regardless of whether the individuals are same-gendered, differently gendered, or nonbinary. The concept of marriage within Paganism is very open-minded.

But that open-mindedness is not always found in local laws, which may restrict which people and how many are allowed to legally marry. The Pagan ritual of handfasting is a welcome option for individuals who may not have the option for their love and relationship to be recognized through legal channels or for those individuals who may not desire such recognition for their relationship. As such, these ceremonies may be public or private.

The concept of handfasting originated in the British Isles during the medieval period and was adopted by modern Pagans for its beautiful symbolism, versatility, and recognition of promises made by the involved parties regardless of the law of the land. Modern rituals frequently involve the people being symbolically bound to each other in the ceremony as they are quite literally bound by their hands. This is done with a cord or ribbon wrapped around their joined hands, representing the joining of their lives together and the weight of the promises they make to each other.

Handfastings may be legally recognized marriage ceremonies if they are conducted by legally ordained Pagan clergy and all local marriage laws are followed (i.e., the procurement of a marriage license, the clergy being registered and vouched for in that county, the recital of any required phrasing as part of the ceremony, the requisite witnesses, the filing of the marriage license, etc.).

Some Pagans opt to have a handfasting with their community after having a legal marriage ceremony, frequently a "courthouse wedding," as part of preserving the privacy of their religious practices from family who may not be accepting of their union or religion or because they are unable to find legally ordained Pagan clergy in their area. The exact ritual for the handfasting is typically crafted specifically for the individuals being bound, being written by themselves, the Pagan minister, or someone whom they trust to do so.

Handfastings are held throughout the year but are frequently associated with Litha, the height of Summer.

Handparting

Handfasting ceremonies are sometimes viewed as having a metaphysical component that binds the spirits of the people joined in union together as much as it binds their lives. In the event that the relationship between these individuals comes to an end, with a divorce if the marriage was legally recognized, a corresponding ceremony to undo the handfasting becomes necessary. This is called a handparting.

Even when such a metaphysical component was not part of the handfasting, a handparting ceremony can provide a welcome sense of closure for all of the parties involved. As part of the ceremony, the handfasting cord will be unknotted and the strands separated, and it may even be burned to further destroy it and symbolize the dissolution of the union.

This ceremony doesn't carry any legal weight. If the union between the individuals was legally recognized, they will need to file for a divorce. Handparting ceremonies are unique to the parties involved and may involve words spoken to express apology, to wish the other individual(s) well in their life and that they may find love again, or simply to express that the union is dissolved and all parties are free to find love as they so seek and desire. This ceremony may be private, or it may be held with the support of the local community.

The ritual of handparting is performed as needed, but it is typically aligned with late Autumn, particularly with the Autumnal Equinox or Samhain, when things that cannot outlast the cold of Winter are sacrificed or naturally die.

Coming of Age

Coming-of-age ceremonies typically refer to ceremonies that commemorate an adolescent's entrance into adulthood. They are often held at the start of puberty; however, the exact timing of that is undefined in Paganism. Consequently, Pagan coming-of-age ceremonies aren't just about becoming an adult but also about becoming the person you know yourself to be and growing into the person you choose to be.

These ceremonies can encompass celebration for coming out as LGBTQIA+ even if that "coming out" is only to yourself and supportive friends. They can also include a ritual celebration in which you take a new name to signify your coming into your own truth and to mark a new chapter of your life. For example, it is common for individuals within some Pagan traditions to take a new name—by which they are then known in their traditions— after deep spiritual experiences that leave them changed. It's also common for trans and nonbinary individuals to take a new name as part of formally embracing who they truly are. In both instances, a coming-of-age ceremony, signifying a new chapter of their lives in which they are, in a sense, reborn, is an appropriate and flexible way to recognize their new reality and the way they will now move in the world.

This rite of passage is not exclusively focused on biological processes, as this presents a limited understanding of how complex and multifaceted human existence is.

Such a focus would also imply an ideal for each of us that is potentially restrictive, inauthentic, and dismissive of personal truths and experiences. That isn't in alignment with Paganism's enduring commitment to inclusivity and the reality of our diversity.

Coming-of-age ceremonies are personal and will differ from one person to the next. There are no common components of these rituals within Paganism, such as vision quests, yet some traditions may feature ritual ordeals as part of these ceremonies. As these ceremonies acknowledge new beginnings, they are typically associated with the Spring Equinox.

Croning and Saging

Paganism embraces the full experience of life and living, not shying away from those aspects that Western society deems undesirable or uncomfortable. So, as much as Pagans celebrate the beginning of life and the beauty of youth, we also celebrate the aging process, recognizing the unique beauty, wisdom, and value that can only be attained with the advancement of years and the accumulation of life experience.

Traditionally, these rites celebrating the twilight of life are called cronings for women and trans women and sagings for men and trans men. At the time of this writing, there is no common name for an equivalent rite for non-binary individuals, but as the Pagan community continues to grow and mature, it is likely that individual traditions will respond to this growing need and an appropriate term will take hold with the community at large.

The timing of these ceremonies is reflective of the individual's experience. They may be timed to correspond to the individual retiring, to the beginning of menopause in individuals who menstruate, to the birth of a first grandchild, or to the acknowledgment of that individual's status as an elder within the community.

In all cases, this ceremony marks the beginning of a new chapter of life for that individual, one in which they may be expected to hold new roles within their tradition, such as those of teacher, guide, or mentor.

These ceremonies may be held whenever deemed necessary but are typically associated with the Autumn Equinox or Samhain. They are typically held within a communal setting; however, there is nothing stopping the solitary Pagan from holding such rituals and ceremonies as they desire and deem necessary as part of their personal practice.

Dedication Rites

Within Paganism, dedication rites entail a promise made by an individual. This promise can encompass many things. Because the context of a dedication rite can vary considerably, you'll likely need to get clarifying information if you are discussing dedication with other Pagans.

Such a dedication may include that individual dedicating themselves to Paganism and making a commitment to study, learn, and grow. It may involve them dedicating to a tradition or group, promising loyalty to that group, such as affirming the core values of that tradition or group, or to keep aspects of the tradition oathbound if it is an initiatory tradition, such as Gardnerian Wicca. Dedication may also be to a new role, such as a Wiccan second-degree initiation. Or it may be as part of an ordination ceremony marking that individual as clergy and minister. Dedication can also be a formal promise one makes to a God or Goddess, taking oaths to that deity and becoming part of that deity's priesthood. In all cases, dedication is not undertaken lightly, as the promises it entails are not easily undone—if at all.

Pagans may undergo numerous dedication rites throughout their practices, with each presenting them with different obligations and roles. Some of these obligations will depend on the role they are assuming as well as the tradition bestowing the role upon them, if applicable. In the case of dedication that includes ordination, those obligations include ensuring that the individual is compliant with local laws so that they are able to perform their duties to the community to their full capacity. (In the US, ordination is a legal certification that can only be conveyed by an established religious organization. It allows that individual to perform legally recognized marriages. Each religious organization determines the requirements for ordination; this is true in Paganism as much as it is in Christianity, Islam, Judaism, or Hinduism, for example.)

Dedication ceremonies may be done whenever they are deemed appropriate and necessary, but they are often associated with Imbolc.

Death

As Paganism recognizes the cyclic nature of life, death is viewed as a necessary and important part of life in Paganism. It is an experience meant to be treated with respect and one in which the dying and departed are to be treated with dignity. This doesn't necessarily make death any easier on the friends and loved ones remaining behind, so the ceremonies Pagans have surrounding death are multifaceted and versatile, crafted for and focused on the dying and departed as much as the living. In both cases, these ceremonies help us cope with the transition of death and soothe the sadness that accompanies it.

Many Pagans believe in reincarnation, so death is seen as a necessary step in order to continue your spiritual journey. While none of us can say with any certainty what happens after death, there is a general view that we find ourselves in the spirit world or Otherworld, where we remain for a period of time. While there, we may be grappling with memories and residual energy from our lives that cling to us, we may reunite with ancestors who help us process our experience and adjust to our new purely energetic state, and we may integrate any lessons from our lives that we learned as part of the overarching journey of our spirit bodies. From there, in time, we may find ourselves reincarnated, our spirit bodies being born within new physical bodies to experience the wonder and beauty of life all over again.

End-of-life and funerary rites vary greatly depending upon the needs and desires of the dying individual and the community they leave behind. There may be a wake, memorial service, and graveside ceremony, but there are no set guidelines. As always, Paganism allows for flexibility with these rituals so they can be tailored to the exact needs of the people for whom they are performed.

Death and funerary rites are typically associated with Samhain; however, they are performed as necessary and desired.

Coming Full Circle

Acknowledging the personal seasons of your life through ritual and celebration serves an important function for Pagans. On the communal level, rites of passage help strengthen a sense of community and remind you that as intense and challenging as life can be, you are not alone in having to face these challenges, and support is available. They help you remain focused on the interconnection we share as well as the similarities we have despite the beautiful diversity of our larger community.

On the personal level, seeing the ways that your life mirrors the Wheel of the Year through cycling seasons provides you another way of feeling a strong connection to the natural world. This can be a great source of comfort when these personal seasons are especially trying, reminding you that we are connected to and part of something larger—both a community and the natural world.

This reminder that all things cycle, that life is meant to be full of change, full of beginnings and endings, helps you view these personal seasons as a part of the wonder of being alive rather than sinking into the despair and frustration that can be so easy to succumb to in life—because you know that no matter how difficult life can get, things will change. The pendulum will swing the other way, and you will enter a new period of growth, in which things slowly become less difficult. Seeing these cycles play out in your life and the ways that you grow and change to meet them reminds you how much you are capable of achieving and helps you remain grateful and open-minded.

CHAPTER 7
Magick

The belief in magick is a prominent part of Pagan practice, even forming the basis of practice in some traditions. Here, we'll look at what magick is, explore why it is important to Pagans, and discuss some of the prominent ways that Pagans work magick.

Creating Change

The worldview of many Pagans is one that paints the world as full and layered. We believe that there are spirits all around us, in all things, and that the Gods can be found within the physical world as easily as They can be found within the spirit world. We see this view of a layered world supported in the layered view we hold of the self, that as the world is physical and spiritual, so, too, are we. It is unsurprising, then, that Pagans believe that as we are able to embrace all levels of ourselves, we are able to be active within all layers of the world.

This manner of being active within the spiritual layer of the world is called magick. There have been many different definitions of magick given over the years by the founders of traditions and magickal orders, as well as countless authors and teachers. What these definitions have in common is the idea that magick is an action. It is something we do, a particular way of moving through the world and interacting with it. When you work magick, you are engaging your spirit body to take hold of and utilize spiritual forces for the purpose of creating change. That change can be many different things, but creating change is the ultimate goal of working magick.

Although magick is worked through the use of spiritual forces, the change that is created is not limited to only occurring in regard to your spirit body or other spiritual forces and beings. For example, it is just as common for Pagans to work magick to help themselves get a better-paying job or to heal from illness as it is for Pagans to work magick to connect more strongly with their ancestors or the Gods.

This magickal mind-set—that we have the ability and are empowered to be fully present and active in the world—underscores Pagan ritual practice even among those who do not actively work magick. This is seen in how each of us is able to honor the Gods and conduct ritual observances on our own and know that the Gods can hear us and that our rituals are effective. Magick is also seen in the importance that signs, synchronicities, omens, and practices like divination are given in the Pagan community, as these are ways you can remain observant of the spiritual forces active within the world around you so you can better respond to them and, thus, live your life in greater harmony with those spiritual forces.

Magick can be both complex and deeply personal, so it isn't surprising that it is embraced differently among Pagan traditions or that there are many unique systems of working magick, such as ceremonial magic and witchcraft. These differing systems provide additional tools, in the form of ritual technology, that help practitioners streamline the process of working magick. These tools help them tap into specific energy currents and even align themselves with particular spirits and deities to increase the efficacy of their magick. These magickal systems may form the backbone of some Pagan traditions, such as witchcraft and Wicca, but they are also practiced in addition to (or adjacent to) the religious structure of a tradition.

Performing Magick

When we speak of "practicing magick," there are many different things to which we may be referring. Magick is the use of spiritual forces to create change, and these deliciously vague parameters mean that all sorts of activities can be and are magickal. We'll explore some of these activities in more detail later in this chapter, but it's important to understand that in terms of practice, magick is nebulous. What distinguishes an activity as magickal as

Magic vs. Magick

The spelling of *magick* with an added "k" is sometimes viewed as a curiosity of modern Paganism, a remnant of when our very young community was rife with revised histories and stories about how "ancient" our very modern traditions and practices are. There is merit in this, for it was during this time of Paganism stretching its limbs and working to establish itself that other, more curious spellings of magick appeared—such as *majik* and *m'j'k*. Yet this spelling of *magick* has been in use for more than 100 years.

Coined by Aleister Crowley in *Magick, Liber ABA, Book 4*, published in the winter of 1912 to 1913, this spelling was meant to distinguish the magick done within spiritual traditions or connected to paranormal phenomena from stage magic. As stage magic is founded on illusion and tricking the mind, this spelling was meant to emphasize the clear distinction that exists between the two in practice and, therefore, avoid the confusion that can arise due to the implication of similarity or the implication that the spiritual practice of magick is equally not real.

In recent years, some Pagans have begun questioning the continued usage of *magick*. In light of such terms as *folk magic* used in common and academic settings without any confusion, it is argued that the need for this distinction does not exist. Considering that much of the magick found within Paganism is based upon European folk magic, this argument appears sound. Yet the prevalence of magic and fantasy themes throughout Western culture has only served to further blur these lines and create a new basis for the distinction. Yes, there are few who would assume an interest in magick means an interest in card tricks and sleight of hand, but it can all too easily be mistaken for an interest in pop-culture magic themes, such as those found in tabletop and computer gaming, cosplay, TV, graphic novels, and digital art.

opposed to ordinary is nothing that can be seen. There are no specific movements or words that make something magickal. Rather, it is the process itself that infuses your actions and transforms something as simple as burning a candle into a ritual that establishes a connection between two people and transfers energy between them, such as for a healing or protection spell.

Although an obvious form of working magick and what comes to mind first for many people, spells are not the be-all-and-end-all of magick. Even in witchcraft traditions, where magick suffuses religious practice, spells make up a very small proportion of the magick worked. This is because of how broad the concept of working magick is and the variety of spiritual activities that fall under its definition.

What do we mean by using spiritual forces to create change? Let's first look at what is meant by spiritual forces. The meaning of this term is twofold. It can mean spiritual beings, such as the Gods and spirits, or it can mean impersonal spiritual energy that flows through and permeates the physical and spirit worlds alike. Magick that involves spiritual beings includes activities focused on engaging with those beings with a goal of creating change. This can easily include activities such as making offerings to the Gods, where the desired change is that we strengthen our connection with Them. It can also include activities such as divination to speak with a spirit or deity, in which the change sought is in the form of knowledge and newfound information.

Magick involving spiritual energy is where things get a bit tricky. Energy is a term that gets tossed around a lot both inside and outside of Paganism. It is the name used for spiritual forces that exist within and without all things. Some go so far as to say that all things are "made of energy." However, this wording dismisses the fact that: the energy we speak of in magick is not the same as the energy we speak of in science; and we don't have any real idea what energy is or any means of figuring that out that aren't dependent upon the use of energy.

But we have a really good idea that something is there and that we are able to manipulate that something in ways that result in changes within ourselves on the physical, mental/emotional, and spiritual levels as well as in the world around us.

When we work magick, there is a basic process involved that helps ensure that the magick worked was successful. Success here isn't based upon what we want happening but upon whether or not the magick was effective. Inability to achieve exactly what we hoped to achieve has more to do with us and how we structured the magick than with magick itself.

The basic process begins with having a clear goal for what you want to achieve. From there, determine the most effective means for achieving that goal. These means may involve a spell or ritual, with items and materials carefully chosen for their correspondence—their energetic relationship to your goal—that are used to tap into desired energies. Or these means may involve embodied activities such as dancing or breath work to raise energy. The energy tapped into or raised is then directed toward the goal, frequently through visualization. From there, the energy is released and sent to its target, where it effects change either directly (i.e., by altering the flow of energy within a person) or by altering the currents of energy surrounding a situation (such as when magick is worked to promote harmony within the workplace).

Let's now look at some common ways that magick is worked.

Visualization

This is the single greatest driving force in magickal practice, with most techniques and methods relying upon or incorporating it in some way. The name *visualization* is a bit of a misnomer, however, as it entails far more than simply picturing something with your mind's eye—which is why visualization is a technique open to those born blind or who have aphantasia (a condition in which you do not possess a functioning mind's eye).

To effectively visualize, it is a full creation or recreation of a scene that is required. So, if you are visualizing as part of journey work and are beginning the session by visualizing yourself standing at the edge of a forest, it isn't enough to *see* yourself standing there. You must create the scene in its entirety: Feel the breeze that rustles the tree leaves and lifts your hair. Smell the pungent notes of pine from the trees, and feel any emotions the scent holds for you. Involve all of your senses; conjure any emotions that arise from being in such a place and experiencing this. Inclusion of all the senses is part of what makes visualization such a potent tool for directing energy and for sending your spirit out of your body and into the spirit world.

Energy Work

Where visualization is the guiding force in magick, energy work is the acting force. Energy within you powers magick and is drawn from tools and objects (such as herbs and stones), or is raised as part of the magickal working—perhaps through breath work, dancing, chanting, or drumming.

Energy can be either pulled or pushed: brought towards us or sent away from us. This difference in energy flow is critical in what you are trying to achieve and is a point that must be considered throughout spell construction and execution.

Practicing basic energy exercises consistently is the most effective way to become more successful with your magick. Five minutes every day of effort focused on feeling and moving energy will go a long way toward building efficacy and increasing sensitivity.

Spells

A spell is a concentrated and deliberate ritual act of magick for the purpose of creating specific change. That deliberateness and the planning that goes into a spell are part of what distinguishes spells from other types of magick. It is important to note that spells *are not* the same as prayers, though it was once common to compare the two. The difference comes down to basic mechanics. With a spell, the burden of success rests entirely on you: You must effectively engage your spirit body to take hold of energy and direct it toward your goal. A prayer, on the other hand, is an act of faith. It may or may not involve a deity, but when it does, it places the burden of success in attaining that goal outside of you and into that deity's hands.

One of the most common forms of spell work is candle magick, which uses a candle as a focal point for raising and directing energy. The candle is charged with energy focused on the goal of the spell and then lit while you maintain focus on the goal of the spell. The candle may be "dressed" in herbs and oil. Although popular, candles are only one way to cast a spell. A spell may involve burning or smoldering herbs, sewing, drawing and painting, dancing, burying things, and the creation of charms.

Journey Work and Astral Travel

Magick embraces the existence of a multilayered world and your ability to be active in each of these layers. One way that you can be active in more than the physical layer is by traveling to the spirit world. Journey work and astral travel are two methods for doing so. They rely upon visualization and a trance state to gently shift your spirit body out of your physical body and into the spirit world.

This trance state may be assisted through chanting, drumming, breath work, dancing or rocking, the use of herbs, and the presence of helping spirits. And it may be undertaken to gather information, to consult with particular spirits and/or deities, or as part of healing work for yourself or others (including nonhuman spirit beings).

Meditation

This is a way of focusing the mind so as to uncover insights and attain a state of mental and emotional relaxation. The intense concentration of meditation needn't be on nothingness. You don't need to be able to empty your mind to benefit from the spiritual and physical benefits of meditation. If you can lose yourself in a task, such as zoning out when doing repetitive tasks like washing the dishes or taking a long walk, you can meditate.

Considering that different religions frequently have very different goals, take care in adopting meditation techniques from other religions and spiritual traditions, as their techniques may be counterproductive. For example, Paganism is generally focused on embracing life and the joy of being physically incarnate. We see the physical world and life as sacred. Techniques that promote severing attachment to the physical world, such as those found in Buddhism, would be ineffective within the context of Paganism.

Herbs, Crystals, and Stones

Pagans hold that all the natural world is sacred, and so natural objects are frequently used in magick and found on Pagan altars for their beauty and energetic potency. Minerals, or what are commonly referred to as "crystals" within magickal practice, and rocks differ in chemical composition, yet both can be powerful allies in magick—including unremarkable stones that you find stuck in the bottom of your shoes.

Herbs are frequently used in both magickal and medicinal contexts, with many Pagans enjoying the process of making incense, powders, soaps, infusions, and oils for use in their magickal practice. Every plant has a use within magick, be it through established correspondences or through the relationship you forge with the spirit of that plant. Don't be too quick to overlook the weeds in your yard; they are more familiar with and effective in the energy currents surrounding you than any herb you could ever buy.

Divination

There are numerous methods of divination, from popular forms such as Tarot and oracle cards to more uncommon methods such as throwing the bones or reading clouds. While these methods differ mechanically, they all work through the use of random variables. Those random variables provide a snapshot of the energy currents surrounding a situation and provide an avenue for you to engage your psychic senses to gain insight into a situation that you otherwise would not have.

Divination can be consulted for more reasons than could ever be compiled. It is a means for you to communicate with the Gods and your ancestors, a way for you to judge whether spell work is necessary or if a situation will resolve itself to your desires, and a tool to gain insight so you can make an informed decision when facing tough choices in life.

Magick in Practice

As already mentioned, magick is a foundation of Pagan religious practice, as it is defined as the belief that we are able, through ritual means and actions, to engage with the spirit world while remaining here, primarily, in the physical world. And so we see that magick is a common component of many Pagan rituals and ceremonies, found in the way that ritual space is delineated, in the way the Gods and other spirits are called to witness and participate in the ritual, and in the way that ritual food and beverages may be first consecrated and then shared.

Of course, magick can be treated quite casually, its use a dominant part of an everyday spiritual practice. But for some Pagans, there is a distinction in how magick is worked when the ritual is primarily devotional in focus. The element of devotion adds a more focused and sometimes serious attitude to the ritual. This is not to imply that working magick is not a serious affair, but that the presence of powerful beings serves to encourage us to be more conscientious about Their time. Many Pagans will correctly maintain a clear distinction between ritual work for the sake of magick and ritual work for the sake of the Gods, choosing to exclude spells and other such acts of magick from ritual centered upon devotion.

Note, though, that there is no firm rule regarding this. Some Pagans actively involve the Gods and other spirits in all aspects of their magick, including spell work. Whatever stance you take is entirely up to you, what you are comfortable with, what you feel your magick requires to be successful, and what the Gods say to you about it.

Altars

The physical center of Pagan magickal practice and worship is frequently an altar. More than just a place to store ritual tools and objects, an altar is a tool in its own right. Its construction (through the placement of ritual objects corresponding to specific energies) creates a portal between the physical and spirit worlds that facilitates the transference of energy—such as when working magick or calling upon the Gods and other spirits.

Many Pagans keep a permanent altar within their home; however, it is not a requirement. The term *altar*, by definition, implies a temporary presence (an altar not in use is more properly called a shrine), so it is perfectly acceptable to erect an altar prior to its use and then dismantle it once done. It is not uncommon for Pagans to have more than one permanent altar within their home. For example, there may be one altar for the Gods of that household, another for that individual's or family's ancestors, and another that is personal to the individual and where they work magick. Many Pagans utilize one altar as a multipurpose space; however, it is considered improper to combine an altar or shrine for your ancestors with one for the Gods or an altar at which you primarily work magick. This is because work with ancestors typically is expansive and intense, requiring its own focused magick as part of honoring those ancestors and resolving ancestral trauma. The mixing of the various energies associated with your ancestors, the Gods, and any spell work is counterproductive and impinges on the respect intended toward these spiritual beings.

Common items found on a Pagan altar include representations of deities (such as statues, paintings, or representative candles); bowls for offerings and libations; ritual tools (such as an athame, wand, or divination tool—see more on these in the following chapter); luminary and offertory candles; photos of ancestors; ongoing spell work; and spirit houses (vessels used to hold spirits in either a temporary or a permanent fashion).

What exactly is found on a Pagan altar depends upon a number of factors. If the altar is created as part of a group ritual, it will follow any guidelines for an altar layout within that tradition. If erected as part of a ritual to honor certain deities at a Sabbat, there will be a number of objects representing something sacred to each deity, as well as objects associated with that Sabbat, such as brightly colored flowers and sun images at Midsummer.

Everything upon an altar holds meaning and purpose, so it is not a place for everyday clutter. Many people find that the states of their altars are often connected to the state of their spiritual health. When they keep their altars well-tended, it is easier to focus and stay motivated in their spiritual practice. When their altars are neglected, collecting dust and incense ash, they are more likely to feel spiritually lethargic and distracted.

To create an altar within your home, consider the purpose of your altar. If you are looking for a place to make offerings and communicate with the Gods, then your altar should hold items that relate to Them and that help you connect with Them. But if it is a working space, a reminder of your spiritual practice, and a representation of the deeper connections you seek, then your altar should reflect that—with room for you to place tools to help you focus during meditation, room for the use of divination tools, and plenty of space to leave ongoing spells and charms. Ultimately, your personal altar is unique to you and should meet your spiritual needs. If you find that you don't require more than a clean space with a single candle and room for a journal to record your thoughts and meditations, then let your altar reflect that.

CHAPTER 8
Symbols and Tools

The language of religion is tied up in symbolism, and modern Paganism is rich with a variety of symbols, associations, and ritual meaning. Some of the most common examples of this symbolism in action are the ritual tools employed by Pagans. In this chapter, we'll look at common Pagan symbols and tools, as well as touch on the complex meaning this symbolism holds through its association with the elements.

Corresponding with the Elements

A significant part of Pagan cosmology is that the world exists in a literal and a symbolic fashion. That symbolic fashion provides a means for us to make better sense of the world and how it operates. This, in turn, facilitates our ability to better operate from the perspective of being multifaceted individuals existing on three levels: the physical body, the mental/emotional body, and the spiritual body.

A fairly common way that many Pagans approach this symbolic view is through the classic five-elements model conceived in ancient Greece. This view allows things to be understood categorically and thematically as made up of five elements, in whole or in part. These elements are Earth, air, fire, water, and spirit. It is important to keep in mind that in this view, and especially where magick is concerned, none of us *is* an element, and our magick is not naturally aligned to one element over others, although we may feel more comfortable with the energy of one or two elements over others. We are each a *compilation* of the elements, made up of each of them in equal amounts.

Earth

Related to the physical Earth, this is the heaviest element and relates to things that are set, unchanging, and unmovable. It also relates to physical fertility, money and wealth, the home, animals, and plants. Earth teaches us the value of commitment, loyalty, and discipline.

It is typically associated with Winter and the colors green, black (think fertile soil), yellow, and brown. In the context of casting a circle (prominent within ceremonial magic, some witchcraft traditions, and some eclectic

Pagan rituals), the Earth element relates to the northern quarter of the circle.

Air

Related to the sky, air is an element of movement and change. It also relates to the mind and mental abilities, as well as communication, divination, and travel. Air teaches you the importance of being open-minded, taking in information, and seeing things in new ways.

A hot and wet element, it is associated with Spring and the color yellow and sometimes white, blue, or gold. In the context of a circle, it relates to the east and is where many magicians, witches, and Pagans will begin casting the circle—as the sun and moon rise in the east.

Fire

Perhaps the most puzzling element, fire relates to the chemical process that we know as fire and the visible component of flame. The element of fire is transformative but also destructive, as anything that is transformed must have its old form destroyed in order for its new form to take shape. Fire relates to the sun and the spark of life and to passion (in the sense of romantic attraction), love, anger, rage, bloodlust, and violence. Fire is also a protective element, as it can keep things at bay, and it can be used for healing in the sense of burning away disease and infection.

Fire is associated with Summer and is described as hot and dry. In the circle, it correlates to the south.

Water

Related to its namesake, the element of water is associated with movement, flexibility, dreams, emotions, the moon, and psychic abilities. Water teaches us to let go and move on.

Viewed as cold and wet, water relates to Autumn, as well as to the spirit's journey from the physical world to the spirit world in death. In the context of ceremonial-style circle casting, water is associated with the west.

Spirit

As nebulous as fire, the element of spirit is frequently misunderstood. It is that animating force within each of us, that bit of us that is enduring and eternal, that transcends personality and physical form.

There are no tools relating to the element of spirit, yet in the context of a ritual circle, the element of spirit is found in the center—where we place our altars and evoke the Gods, who are the ultimate embodiment of spirit.

The element of spirit reminds us that just as we are multifaceted and exist on multiple levels, so, too, does the natural world. The spirit element keeps us focused on how much larger the world is than we can see, hear, and touch. It reminds us of the sacredness we each possess, the sacredness found throughout the natural world.

A DIFFERENT ELEMENTAL APPROACH

Not all Pagans work with or embrace this model. Some Pagans, such as Druids and traditional witches, embrace a similar yet different concept of land, sky, and sea in which the union of these three creates a liminal space that facilitates communication with the Gods, Otherworld travel, and magick.

About Correspondences

It's also important to remember that even though elemental and other correspondences (such as for happiness, protection, or wealth) can be determined for any object, correspondences are not to be treated as a list of ingredients or a checklist of things you must have in order to achieve X.

Correspondences are a starting point for understanding the intrinsic energy of an object or thing and its relationship with other objects, things, and forces. Looking at a correspondence list and choosing whatever herbs, stones, and deities relate to a magickal focus and then using that as the basis for a ritual, magick, or spell *will not* be as effective as if you take the time to understand the energies within each object and how they operate in the context of that object. The Gods do not take kindly to being treated as correspondences. Remember, They are people. Just because a deity is strongly associated with warriorship or the hearth doesn't mean that They are willing to help you with magick focused on protecting your home—regardless of how many similar "correspondences" you strew across your altar.

Pagan Symbols

Within Paganism you'll find a considerable variety of symbols. Many of these symbols were originally found in ancient cultures, while others are modern. There is no one tradition within Paganism that incorporates all of these symbols, and some are exclusive to certain traditions. Solitary eclectic Pagans tend to make use of symbols as they hold relevance within their practice, to the Gods they honor, and to any magick they may be working, so their use of symbols may be very fluid and situationally dependent.

Pentacle

A five-pointed star (pentagram) bound by a circle, the pentacle is an ancient symbol found in many different cultures and religions, including Christianity. It is apotropaic, meaning it is a symbol of protection. It is also the generally recognized symbol of Wicca, relating to the element of Earth.

Triple Moon

With two crescent moons on either side of a circle, the triple moon symbol represents the lunar cycle in the northern hemisphere (as it shows the waxing, full, and waning phases) as well as goddesses associated with the moon. It can be used to draw in lunar energies or to help with focus in working with lunar deities.

Eye of Horus

Also known as the *wadjet*, the Egyptian eye of Horus is depicted as a right eye. It is associated with protection, the lunar-associated god Horus, good health, and power.

Eye of Ra

Similar to the eye of Horus, the eye of Ra is depicted as a left eye. It is associated with the solar-aligned god Ra, good fortune, and creation.

Ankh

A cross with the upper vertical bar formed as a loop, the Egyptian ankh represents life and the power to maintain and restore life. It sometimes represents air and breath (especially as in "the breath of life").

Hekate's Wheel

Also known as the *strophalos*, Hekate's wheel is a common symbol among devotees of the goddess Hekate, representing Her as a triform goddess (not a *triple* goddess). It is used as a focal point in ritual, as part of evoking Her in workings, and as a representation of one's devotion to Her.

Triquetra

Also called a trefoil knot or trinity knot, the triquetra originated among Celtic peoples, likely in the seventh century. In modern Paganism, it is used to represent feminine deities; land, sky, and sea; and the modern concept of maiden, mother, and crone as used by Dianic Wiccans.

Triskele

Comprised of three interlocking spirals, the triskele is an ancient Celtic symbol representing movement and motion, especially cycles. Modern Pagans may also use it to represent the three levels of the self; land, sky, and sea; and any other particular meaningful association with the number three.

Septagram

A seven-pointed star, it is sometimes called an elven or faery star. Its seven points are given a variety of associations, particularly the seven directions (north, east, south, west, above, below, and within) and the seven planets.

Spiral Goddess

A modern symbol representing divine feminine energy, the spiral goddess taps into the procreative powers associated with women who menstruate. The spiral on the belly is indicative of the creative powers of the uterus as connected to pregnancy. It is a favored symbol among feminist witches and Pagans.

Labyrinth

An ancient symbol of various forms, the labyrinth combines the wholeness of the circle with the inward/outward movement of the spiral. In Paganism, it can be used to enter a trance state, by walking a labyrinth or by tracing a small labyrinth with one finger or a stylus. It is especially useful for finding answers to problems by seeking a way through the maze.

Air

The alchemical symbol for air is frequently used to represent the element of air. It is depicted as a masculine, upward-pointing triangle bisected by a horizontal line. This symbol allows you to tap into the elemental qualities of air: intellect, communication, and travel.

Earth

Depicted as a feminine, downward-pointing triangle bisected by a horizontal line, the alchemical symbol for Earth is often used to represent the element of Earth and to tap into its qualities of strength, stability, and constancy.

Fire

In alchemy, the element of fire is depicted as a masculine, upward-pointing triangle. This symbol is common throughout Paganism. It is used as a simple means of tapping into the transformative and protective qualities of the fire element.

Water

A feminine, downward-pointing triangle, this symbol also comes to Paganism from alchemy. It is an effective way to tap into the water element's qualities of fluidity and psychicness.

Horned God

A circle topped with an upward-pointing crescent, the horned god symbol is modern, coming into Paganism from Wicca, where it represents the masculine deity. It is a symbol of divine masculine energy and the creative, protective, and wild energies often associated with such traits.

Helm of Awe (Ægishjálmr)

An ancient Germanic symbol, the helm of awe is a symbol of protection and power, believed to be able to strike adversaries with terror so as to prevent them from attacking. It is often used in Paganism as a symbol of physical, mental, and spiritual protection.

Tree of Life

A common symbol throughout many ancient cultures, the tree of life is also known as the world tree and by the name Yggdrasil in Heathenry. Its meanings are varied, representing a connective force linking the physical world and the spirit world, immortality, and fertility.

Rod of Asclepius

Originating in ancient Greece, this symbol depicts the rod held by the god Asclepius. It is frequently confused with the caduceus. A rod with a single snake twined about it, the rod of Asclepius represents medicine and healing.

Caduceus

Often confused with the rod of Asclepius, the caduceus is a rod twined with two serpents and sometimes depicted with wings at the top, carried by the god Hermes. It is associated with commerce and business.

Ouroboros

Depicted as a snake (sometimes a dragon) eating its own tail and forming a circle, this symbol is common within Western esotericism. It represents wholeness, eternity, and the cycle of life, death, and rebirth.

Thor's Hammer (Mjölnir)

A Norse symbol found within modern Heathenry, Mjölnir is the war hammer carried by the god Thor. It is a symbol of protection and is also used to denote a devotee of Thor, in addition to being used as a representative symbol of Heathenry in general.

Valknut

Although the name is modern, this symbol of three inter-locking triangles is common in ancient Norse mythology. The name means "slain warrior knot," while the symbol itself is associated with Odin and protection.

Spiral

The spiral is an ancient symbol found in numerous cultures. In modern Paganism, it represents creative energy, movements, and cycles. It is often used in magick to draw energy in or send it out, depending on whether the spiral is drawn in a clockwise or counterclockwise direction.

Awen

The representative symbol of modern Druidry, the awen symbolizes divine inspiration. It is a modern symbol, and its three lines are also viewed as representing the three domains of land, sky, and sea.

Pagan Tools

Remembering that Paganism encompasses many different traditions—traditions that sometimes have very little in common aside from shared modern history—it is impossible to predict what any one Pagan may use as far as religious tools. Many Pagans will have only a small selection of tools, sticking to what is most relevant to their practice. Not all Pagans practice magick, so these individuals will frequently use fewer tools.

Many of the tools in the following list originated within ceremonial magic and have found their way into the larger Pagan sphere due to the popularity of eclectic Wicca during the nineties. For this reason, some of these tools will be unusual outside of Wiccan or Wiccan-inspired traditions, while some are typical only in religious and secular witchcraft practice.

Sword

Common within ceremonial magic and traditional forms of Wicca, yet rarely seen outside of them, the sword is a masculine tool corresponding to either fire or air. It is a defensive tool, used for banishing, commanding spirits, and casting the circle (an energetic construct used as part of delineating ritual space).

Bell

Associated with the element of air, the bell is used in various witchcraft traditions as a tool for cleansing and purification, as well as for banishing spirits and faeries. The tongue of the bell is sometimes viewed as masculine, while the bell itself is feminine.

Besom

A ritual broom used solely by witches, the besom is used to remove unwanted energies from an area as part of cleansing rituals. It is associated with either fire or air and is sometimes leaped over as part of handfasting ceremonies.

Athame

A black-handled knife found within ceremonial magic and Wicca, the athame typically has a dull blade, as it is not used for physical cutting. It corresponds to either fire or air, depending on tradition, and is a primary tool used for directing energy.

Wand

Belonging to both ceremonial magic and Wicca, the wand is made from a living branch cut from a tree. Some traditions will modify the branch by embedding a metal rod within it, while others will inscribe symbols upon its surface. Aligned with either fire or air, the wand is a tool of invocation and evocation, used to draw energies and spirits. However, some witches have come to use the wand as an alternative to the athame.

Chalice or Cup

Corresponding to the element of water, the chalice is a ritual cup found in both ceremonial magic and Wicca. It enjoys practical use in many Pagan traditions on occasions when a ritual beverage is shared among participants. Some traditions view it as a symbol of divine feminine energy.

Cauldron

A tool of transformation, change, and inspiration, the cauldron is rarely found outside witchcraft traditions and Druidry. It is associated with both fire and water and may be used to hold liquid water or actual flames as part of ritual.

Pentacle

A small disc made of metal, stone, or wax, the pentacle is inscribed with various symbols, sometimes (but not always) including the symbol of the pentacle. It is a traditional tool of Wicca, used to represent the element of Earth and to consecrate tools and direct energy.

Staff

Found within various Pagan traditions, the staff is a large piece of wood, generally about the height of the person to whom it belongs. It may be carved or decorated. It corresponds to either the fire or the air element.

Candles

A versatile tool ubiquitous in Paganism, candles are used to represent the element of fire. However, they are more commonly used as a primary tool in magick, as representations of deities, as focal points in magick and ritual, and as luminaries for the altar.

Book of Shadows

Found within Wicca, a Book of Shadows is a personal book that contains all of the lore and rites of that particular Wiccan tradition up to the degree into which that individual has been initiated. It also includes personal lore and witchcraft material, such as documentation of spells, herb lore, and divinatory readings.

Crystals, Stones, and Minerals

A common component of magick, stones and minerals—including salt—are used due to the intrinsic energies within them. Admittedly, many Pagans prefer the crystalline forms of minerals; however, many of these "crystals" have been cut and shaped, as they are not naturally found that way. From the animist perspective, the spirits within these stones can be spoken with, a relationship can be forged with them, and their help can be requested in magick.

Robe

Pagans of many traditions, especially clergy, will wear robes during ritual to signify the sacredness of the ritual, to adopt the necessary difference in mind-set for the ritual, and to denote their role. Outside of Druidry, where robes are traditionally white, there are few standards for what Pagan ritual wear or robes must look like.

Censer

A small dish for holding charcoal discs for smoldering incense, the censer is a practical tool that enjoys considerable use by many Pagans. Incense is a common component in ritual and magick. The censer is associated with the element of air. It is a tool of transference and movement.

Hammer

Found exclusively within Heathenry, the hammer is symbolic of Mjölnir and is used in ritual to convey blessings.

Stang

The stang is sometimes used interchangeably with the staff, but it is generally a tool found primarily within traditional witchcraft traditions (not to be confused with Wicca) and differs in that it has forked branches at the top (typically two, so that the stang resembles the letter Y) or features the skull of a horned animal at the top, such as a deer or goat, rather than possessing forking branches. It is a versatile tool used at the center of rituals, with the altar being built around and upon it. It represents the world tree and is also used within magick.

Crane Bag

A practical tool found in Druidry, the crane bag holds all other ritual tools, such as small instruments, divination tools, incense, and candles, as well as a lighter or matches, a utility knife, and maybe even the Druid's car keys.

CHAPTER 9
Pagan Rituals

Since Paganism celebrates the uniqueness of the individual and the strength of diversity, it is no surprise that each person practices Paganism in their own way. Yet religious observance in the form of rituals is a common part of Pagan practice regardless of tradition. Here, we'll look at the ways that Pagans practice their religions and the general steps that make up most Pagan rituals.

Paganism in Practice

Every Pagan's practice is unique to them. Even for two people who belong to the same tradition, the ways they approach their religions day-to-day will differ. Also, within the framework of a shared religious context, people have different spiritual needs. How religions are embraced and embodied will be different for every individual, depending upon their specific needs and predilections.

While no two people will practice Paganism in the same way, there are still some generalities that can be established for what Pagan practice can look like and some common ways that Pagans engage in their personal practices.

Prayer

The subject of prayer is a bit contentious in Paganism. Some people find it to be a rewarding and valuable part of their practices, while others consider it needless, as we are each able to engage in direct communication with the Gods. Yet, for some, prayer can be a useful piece of religious technology, helping strengthen feelings of connection and resolve during spiritual challenges. Whether, and how often, a Pagan prays and to Whom is entirely up to them.

Discussion

While Pagans vary in how much they come together in person, we are a community that has very much taken to the Internet and rely upon it as a way to learn, share, and strengthen our community and individual practices. Between blogs, community sites, news sites, and hundreds of thousands of Pagans visible on social media, an active and thriving Pagan community is available to us all, regardless of where we live. A few minutes spent on any search engine can easily yield more results than you could ever hope to sort through.

Worship

Devotion to the Gods can take many forms; it isn't merely relegated to formal ritual in front of an altar. We can honor the Gods and strengthen our connection to Them when we think of Them and research the ways that ancient peoples perceived and honored Them just as much as we do when we make offerings to Them. And those offerings can take many forms. They can be food and drink, but they can also be in the form of embodied activities such as song and dance, art, volunteering at a shelter, time spent in nature picking up trash and restoring the landscape, archery, handcrafts, or running. In this way, Pagans may worship the Gods daily and not just on recognized religious holidays.

Learning

Actively learning about our traditions and Gods through study, sharing, and direct experience makes up the bulk of Pagan practice for many people. The Pagan community is very much a community with a deep love of books and reading, and study is highly encouraged. Critical thinking, self-analysis, and personal growth and enrichment are highly valued and encouraged by leaders and general members alike.

Divination

Divination is a way for us to check in on the energy currents active in our lives, and many Pagans utilize divination on a daily basis. More than just fortune telling, divination is a way for you to learn more about yourself, to communicate with spirits such as your ancestors, and to gain another perspective on important issues you're facing. Tarot, oracle cards, runes, ogham, throwing the bones, pendulums, scrying, and geomancy are a few types of divination Pagans may use.

Meditation

The ease of meditation, paired with the calm and clarity of mind that it brings, makes it a common practice for many Pagans. Meditation may be the basis of daily practice as well as being incorporated into solitary ritual observances for the lunar cycle, Sabbats, and other holidays. It is an adaptive practice that all can engage in regardless of tradition.

Magick

For many Pagans, working magick forms a significant part of their spiritual practice. This may look like daily energy exercises to strengthen psychic skills and sensitivity, regular astral travel, energy work as part of a larger energy-healing practice, the creation of charms and talismans for oneself and others, or simple enchantment of meals for good health and vitality.

Gathering

Most Pagans practice as solitaries, and many do so by choice, yet it is also common for Pagans to come together as a community in a variety of ways. Weekly or monthly study groups, casual get-togethers (called "moots"), and seasonal festivals aligned to the Sabbats provide a way for you to feel the bonds of community while still maintaining a strong feeling of autonomy in your practice. However, some Pagans will never gather with others; this doesn't negatively impact their ability to be Pagan.

The Goals of Gathering

When planning a group ritual, there are a number of factors to keep in mind. Regardless of their purpose, group rituals are first and foremost for the group. Even in a Heathen blót, for example, in which the purpose of the ritual is to sacrifice to the Gods, the ritual is a means for those individuals to come together as a community and honor the Gods. The ritual must be designed to accommodate the needs of the individuals involved; otherwise they can't fulfill the purpose of the ritual.

These accommodations include making sure:

- **the ritual has clearly defined start and end times;**

- **the ritual is hosted at an easily accessible location;**

- **there are plenty of chairs (with arms and without arms) available for people who can't stand for long periods of time;**

- **there is a handicap-accessible bathroom available and stocked with plenty of toiletries;**

- **all ritual food is labeled with the ingredients noted for those who have food allergies;**

- **and paper copies of the ritual format and any spoken parts are available for everyone.**

An important part of group ritual, too, is ensuring that everyone knows what is going to happen before the ritual begins. There is no spiritual benefit to anyone involved in deciding mid-ritual to change things up and call in new spirits or deities or suddenly take the participants on an intense journey to the Underworld. This not only betrays trust but also betrays consent. We each have a right to decide what spirits and deities we engage with and in what magickal work we want to participate. Being up-front ahead of time respects everyone's right of choice and also ensures that everyone is focused on the purpose of the ritual—both of which go a long way to making for a successful ritual.

Ritual Steps and Procedures

When Pagans come together for religious observance, the ceremony or worship service is frequently called a *ritual*. In the general sense, a ritual is any set of prescribed steps that can be faithfully repeated to accomplish the same goal. While this term can (in an anthropological sense) be used to apply to magickal work, it almost exclusively refers to solitary or group religious observances.

However, not all traditions refer to their formal religious observances as rituals. Instead, it may be more common to refer to the ritual by the specific category it falls under within that tradition. For example, in Heathenry, rituals frequently take the form of a blót or symbel, as noted in chapter 2 (page 20), and are referred to as such. These are rituals to sacrifice to and honor the Gods and to strengthen the community, respectively. It's important to also note that exact steps for a ritual may vary depending upon the tradition. We'll explore general ritual steps shortly, but it isn't unusual for a tradition to not include all of these steps or to include additional steps. How those steps are performed can also vary greatly.

Although a ritual generally follows set steps, in practice, it can be quite spontaneous and organic for solitary Pagans. There will be times when you will be out in nature and feel moved by the beauty of the place and very connected to the Gods. This is a perfect moment to recognize the sacredness of the land and honor your connection to the Gods through an impromptu ritual, perhaps involving an offering of your water, a song, or a simple moment of quiet meditation to open yourself to the presence and words of the Gods, as well as any land spirits.

Ritual is an important part of Pagan practice and a way for you to formally acknowledge the sacred in your life. It is a way of reaffirming faith, as it is a means for you to focus intently on your connection to forces much larger than yourself. It is a means for you to honor and be with the Gods, to raise energy to effect changes in your life and the world around you. It is a means for you to come together with community and work to create change on a local and global level, to confront the darkest parts of yourself and bring them into the light so you can heal and grow. Ritual is how you stand in a world that can feel so very hectic and choking at times and reclaim your right to live with purpose and with a focus on the sacred.

For these reasons, the rituals you perform can be spontaneous and from the heart, they can be carefully written and memorized beforehand, or they can be read from a book. There is no right or wrong way to do ritual. Mistakes can happen, yes, but your Gods are far more concerned with your efforts and what you choose to do than with whether or not you remembered to bless the ritual wine before pouring it out.

As long as you approach ritual for what it is—a way for you to touch the sacred—you cannot do it wrong. But, nonetheless, be sure to turn off your phone before a group ritual begins. How focused can you be on calling the Gods and raising energy if you're trying to get the perfect photo of the altar? Above all, be present for the ritual; after all, that's why you're there in the first place.

Grounding, Centering, and Purifying

Prior to ritual, it is customary in many traditions to perform some sort of purification of the participants and of the space in which the ritual is held (if held indoors; outdoor spaces do not require purification or cleansing). This may involve the use of smoldered herbs, such as in incense, to individually bathe the space and the participants in order to remove miasma (ritual pollution and energy that could prove disruptive in the ritual). It can also involve sprinkling the space and participants with consecrated water, using a bell to energetically cleanse the area, or sprinkling consecrated salt around the ritual space.

Some groups and individuals may also perform energetic exercises such as grounding, where the individual establishes an energetic link between themselves and the Earth below and between themselves and the sky above, creating a complete energetic circuit. This has the effect of balancing the energies within the body and removing excess energy. From there, centering exercises may be done. These move your focus from being too externally or too internally focused and instead place your awareness at that point where the physical body, the mind and emotions, and the spirit body meet. This induces a calm yet attentive state that is conducive to ritual.

When these exercises are done in a group setting, they help ensure that everyone is approaching the ritual in a similarly focused state, with their attention and energy ready to conduct the ritual, perform any magick, and engage with whatever spiritual powers or beings may be called into the ritual.

Delineating Sacred Space

The ritual typically begins with the creation of sacred space. This phrasing can seem odd, as Pagans hold that all of the natural world is sacred, yet when we create sacred space as part of a ritual, we are setting that space aside from the everyday and focusing energies toward the purpose of the ritual. As rituals are just as likely to be held indoors as outdoors, this action is helpful in energetically transforming an indoor space, such as a living room, into a temple space.

The sacred space may be physically marked, such as through the placing of stones around the perimeter, or it may be energetically marked, such as by casting a circle or creating a nemeton (a sacred space), or both. In this way, energy is projected out of the body (using your hand or a ritual tool such as an athame, wand, staff, stang, or sword) while tracing a circle around the perimeter of the ritual space, moving in a clockwise direction. This creates an energetic ring that then extends into a sphere, setting the ritual space between the worlds. The casting of a circle or creation of a nemeton has the effect of creating an energetic boundary, changing the way that participants experience time, and aids in maintaining concentration and focus.

Not all traditions will create sacred space in such a fashion, and those that do may not do so for every ritual. Some traditions will instead bless or hallow the space to make it fit for the Gods but will not go to such lengths to alter the energy of the space.

Calling the Powers

Once the ritual space has been prepared, through purification and creation of sacred space, any spiritual powers who are desired to be present for the ritual are called and invited into that space. In Wiccan rituals, this will typically begin by calling the Elements: spirits of Earth and direction of north, spirits of Air and direction of east, spirits of Fire and direction of south, and spirits of Water and direction of west. Druids may call the powers of land, sky, and sea to bless and watch the ritual. Heathens may call upon the land wights (land spirits) and ancestors to join and be honored as part of the ritual.

Next, any deities who are being honored are called. Note that the word *invocation* is sometimes used to describe this; however, *to invoke* a god or spirit is to call it into your body, a form of ritual possession that is found in some Pagan traditions. The word *evoke* is the proper term, as it means to call a spirit or deity to you but outside of your body, such as when we invite the Gods to be present during ritual.

These spirits and deities may be called to the ritual by reciting hymns, poetry, or a short verse. In a group ritual, these spiritual powers may be called by officiating priests (a nongendered term), or each spirit or deity may be called by a different person. In a solitary ritual, you will be calling all spirits and deities on your own, using whatever means you feel most comfortable with or that They require of you (in the case of the Gods).

Purpose of the Ritual

Once every necessary and desired spirit and/or deity is present, the purpose of the ritual is then carried out. Remembering that ritual is a general term for a Pagan religious service, what happens at this point can vary greatly. It could involve the celebration of a rite of passage, perhaps the dedication of a new member to that group. Or it could involve ritual theater as part of celebrating one of the Sabbats, such as a dramatic play inspired by the Eleusinian mysteries and performed at the Autumnal Equinox.

In many traditions, this is when the Gods are honored. Sacrifices, in the form of offerings and libations, will be made with great display. This may be done as a group, with the officiating priests making the offering for everyone, or with every participant sacrificing something, such as pouring a libation of wine or throwing a handmade object into a fire.

This is also when any magick is worked. In traditions that embrace Oracular work, the Gods will be invoked into the body of a spirit worker or medium and then speak through that person's lips, delivering guidance and wisdom. The group may also work together to raise energy toward a common goal, perhaps sending healing energy to one of their members or working to create change on a larger scale, such as to influence lawmakers on issues relating to the land and marginalized peoples. Divination may also be worked at this time, perhaps through one member of the group interpreting drawn runes while in trance. Magick may also be worked to help the participants be in better harmony with the Earth in their everyday lives, giving them strength to live their values and make lifestyle changes that benefit the land.

Blessing and Sharing

A common part of group rituals is the sharing of food and drink. In some traditions, this is a way for us to express gratitude for the abundance of the Earth and to communally acknowledge the ways in which the Gods are active in our lives. There is also something so beautifully intimate about sharing food and drink with each other. It creates bonds where none had been and strengthens bonds that otherwise have grown weak. In passing food and drink among us, we acknowledge the bonds of community that are founded in the frailty of life, in the knowledge that it is through community that any of us survives and thrives. It is a moment in which we experience one another as true equals.

This food and drink are typically first blessed. They may be placed upon the altar or held aloft in the air, whichever is practical, and a blessing by the Gods called upon them. In a solitary ritual, you can do this by holding your hands over the food and/or drink and asking that the Gods bless them, using these or similar words:

[Deity], bless this food and drink that, as it nourishes my body, Your presence in my life may nourish my mind and spirit.

Some traditions may recite words as the food and drink are passed, such as telling each other, "May you never hunger/thirst," to reflect the bounty of the Earth and call a blessing onto each other that we may each always know and experience that bounty.

Thanking and Farewells

The purpose of the ritual having been fulfilled, the ritual will begin to come to a close in much the same way as it began, undoing the ritual steps until the ritual space has been returned to its usual state. The Gods will be thanked for attending and bearing witness to the ritual. Some traditions make a point of thanking the Gods and bidding Them farewell with the words "Go if you must, stay if you will" to emphasize that we cannot tell the Gods what to do and that Their presence is always desired in our lives.

Other spirits and beings who have been called to the ritual space will then also be thanked for coming. This may involve additional libations and offerings, such as water or incense. Some spirits may require actual sending away, where they are politely pushed out of the ritual space using the same energetic techniques as when they were called. This may not be as necessary in outdoor rituals, but when working within your home, knowing that every spirit called for the ritual is gone and out of your home can be comforting (after all, we all like having our own space).

If sacred space was created, it will now be taken down. For a cast circle, it will be opened by walking the circle counterclockwise and pulling the energy of the circle back into you, using the same ritual tool or none at all. Some traditions may recite words to denote that the ritual has come to a close and calling a final blessing onto the participants, perhaps that all may depart in peace or that all may leave with the love of the Gods in their hearts. (Note that there is no set verbiage or protocol across all traditions.)

CHAPTER 10

Discovering a Spiritual Life

Connecting with other Pagans through shared tradition adds a layer to our spiritual practices that helps us feel grounded within our practices and part of a community. In this chapter, we'll explore the ways that Pagans connect with each other and offer guidance on how to find a tradition to focus on in your individual studies and practice.

Finding Your Tradition

With so many traditions under the Pagan umbrella, determining whether you should focus on one tradition exclusively can be difficult—never mind choosing which tradition to explore. Each tradition offers different benefits, based upon the values and spiritual relationships it emphasizes, such as placing stronger emphasis on ancestors, one's local landscape, or certain deities. Each also has different requirements for its members. Some traditions only allow for group practice, requiring initiation into that tradition and group and then a minimum attendance at group meetings. Depending upon the choices you've made for your life, meeting the requirements of such traditions may be unrealistic no matter how committed you are to the tradition. Other traditions may be more flexible, being comprised predominantly of solitaries who follow a general structure for rituals and holidays.

On the other hand, you may feel strongly called to one tradition in particular. Perhaps you know someone who practices that tradition and have seen the value that it brings to their life. Or perhaps certain Gods have begun making appearances in your life, making the traditions that honor Them a good place to start. You may even have begun exploring a tradition, using it as a starting point to provide structure for practice while you study and learn more about yourself and your spiritual needs.

While the need to belong can be a powerful influence in our lives, know that you are not required to be part of any tradition in order to be Pagan. Not only are most Pagans solitary, but they also are eclectic, not belonging to any tradition but still having rich and rewarding religious practices that meet their spiritual needs and encourage them to grow and become better people. It's also not uncommon to find that your spiritual interests change as you grow and learn more. You may find yourself first drawn to one tradition but then easing into an eclectic practice, only to find yourself drawn to a very different tradition later. This exploration and moving among traditions is encouraged, as Pagans recognize that there is no one tradition, let alone religion, that is right for all people. Search, explore, discover, and find. Your spiritual journey is your own.

Should you seek a tradition, however, know that aside from initiatory traditions, such as within Wicca, most traditions do not have rigorous requirements for membership. It is enough to say "I am a Druid" or "I am a Heathen" and then follow the general ritual formats to observe the holidays of that tradition and engage with the spirits and deities that they focus on. No tradition requires formal membership or payment of dues. However, some larger organizations within certain traditions, such as the Order of Bards, Ovates, and Druids (OBOD), *do* require membership fees that help them exist on such a large scale. Smaller groups within traditions may ask for donations to help cover costs for meetings and group rituals, but, in general, it does not cost money to be Pagan.

Connecting with the Self

In some regards, Paganism can be seen as a collection of religions driven by spiritual searching. A desire for greater understanding of the world around you serves as encouragement to explore yourself and your connections to the Earth, the Gods, and other people. Collectively, this searching propels Pagans forward, helping the traditions and community mature and deepen those connections. Individually, this searching helps you better understand yourself and your spiritual needs. This, in turn, helps you create a spiritual practice that is responsive, nurturing, and grounded within a tradition that best meets your needs while challenging you to grow and become a better person.

This process of searching and connecting with yourself never truly ends. While this can be frustrating at times, as you may struggle to feel like you have found your "path," this searching keeps you open to new discoveries and experiences. This means that, regardless of the direction your practice takes, you can be secure in the fact that you are never headed in the wrong direction. Your path is always firmly beneath your feet, and although it may shift and turn, and your focus—and even your traditions—may change, every step forward is a way for you to learn new skills, explore new topics, and gain valuable spiritual experiences that help you learn and grow.

To guide your searching and help you find a direction in which to focus in your Paganism, consider the following questions. Try journaling your responses, as this will give you ample time to think through the questions, yielding greater insight.

What does your ideal practice look like? Are you practicing with others or as a solitary? If you practice with others, how involved are you in that group? Does this group offer training, or are they more casual and focused on building community rather than religious practice? How do you feel when engaging in this ideal practice? What does your life look like as a result of this ideal practice?

What are your current spiritual goals? Are there skills you're interested in cultivating? Are there things you would like to learn or areas of study that interest you? What is required for you to move closer to your vision for your ideal spiritual practice, and how can you begin making progress toward that vision now? What obstacles stand between you and your goals? What can you do to successfully overcome those obstacles? What are your current spiritual struggles, and how do you feel Paganism can best support you in those struggles?

What are your values? What are the qualities or traits that you find most admirable in a person and that you wish to cultivate more strongly within yourself? Are there any particular social or environmental issues that are of particular importance to you? What qualities do you consider essential for you to belong to a religious group or tradition? What qualities are deal breakers that would prevent you from joining a religious group or tradition?

Opening the Door to Paganism

To help you further determine which Pagan tradition is a good fit for you, consider the following questions. While this quiz cannot guarantee that a tradition best meets your spiritual needs, it can help you narrow your options and perhaps consider a tradition you might otherwise have dismissed.

1. **What is your ideal level of guidance and structure?**

   A. General framework but, ultimately, responsible for myself
   B. I don't need anyone telling me what to do
   C. General framework but with an emphasis on divine inspiration to guide me
   D. I just need some ideas for celebrating holidays
   E. I look forward to the experience I'll gain in finding my own way
   F. The more it's based on how the ancients did things, the better

2. **Are you interested in formal training and/or a teacher?**

   A. Absolutely! I'd love a teacher, even if only temporarily
   B. Training for what?
   C. I'm not necessarily against it, but it's not a requirement
   D. I'm not against the occasional workshop, but I don't need a teacher
   E. Teaching and guidance can come in many forms
   F. I'd rather go to the source and find out for myself

3. **How interested in magick are you?**

   A. Magick is a lifestyle that connects us more deeply to the natural world
   B. I believe that magick is possible, but I'm not overly interested in practicing
   C. Magick permeates our world and is a means for us to be in harmony with the world
   D. I enjoy working magick, but I really only dabble
   E. Magick is a powerful tool for healing and growth
   F. I'm not very interested

4. **How important to you is deepening your connection to the land and its spirits?**

   A. It is an inseparable part of Pagan practice for me
   B. I honor the spirits of the land, but I don't interact with them directly
   C. Living in harmony with the land and its spirits is essential
   D. It's important to me, but it could be a stronger focus
   E. I work in partnership with the land and its spirits
   F. I'm more interested in the role the Gods play in the natural world

5. **Are strong relationships with your ancestors an important part of your spiritual practice?**

   A. I work with—or want to work with—a variety of spirits
   B. We are nothing without the people we come from
   C. Community plays a vital role in my practice
   D. I honor my ancestors at Samhain, but that's about it
   E. The struggles our ancestors faced continue to affect us; healing them heals us
   F. I honor or wish to more frequently honor my ancestors

6. **Do you prefer solitary practice?**

   A. Group practice and personal practice go
   hand in hand
   B. It would be nice to find a like-minded group;
   community is important
   C. It would be nice to find a like-minded group, but
   it's not essential
   D. I prefer to work alone and like to do my
   own thing
   E. Group practice is unnecessary for what I do
   F. It would be nice to find a like-minded group, but
   I'll honor the Gods regardless

7. **What do you think about political activism
   and religious practice?**

   A. They go hand in hand
   B. I stay informed on issues and vote; that's enough
   C. My religious beliefs influence how I vote
   D. They occasionally intersect
   E. They inform each other
   F. Separation of church and state benefits
   all religions

8. **Is there a particular pantheon of deities to
   Whom you are drawn?**

   A. Not an entire pantheon, but there are a few
   specific deities
   B. Norse and Germanic pantheon
   C. Ancient Irish pantheon
   D. Not really; I prefer to work with deities as needed
   E. I honor and engage with the Gods as we
   cross paths
   F. Any ancient pantheons, such as the Celtic, Greek,
   Roman, and Egyptian pantheons

9. **Do your personal values drive what you look for in a tradition?**

   A. Yes, the values of the tradition should be explicitly stated

   B. Values are important, but our actions define our character

   C. Shared values influence the quality of our relationships

   D. I'm still exploring my values and/or am not sure I'm interested in a tradition

   E. I'm more strongly focused on purpose

   F. Essential values are consequent on right behavior by the Gods

10. **How important is it to follow ritual procedure?**

   A. I will either follow it perfectly or rely entirely on intuition

   B. It's really just a guideline

   C. A gentle framework facilitates inspiration and connection

   D. My procedure is my own

   E. A strong framework serves as a tool that facilitates practice

   F. Meaning isn't as important as that we act and do

Answer Key

Mostly A's
Wicca or Witchcraft

Mostly B's
Heathenry

Mostly C's
Druidry

Mostly D's
Eclectic Pagan

Mostly E's
Shamanism

Mostly F's
Celtic, Greek, or other Gods-focused
polytheistic tradition

Finding Your Community

Although the lack of a central organizing body within Paganism can feel like an impediment to finding your place within the greater community, this feature encourages a plethora of groups and organizations on both the local and the national level. This allows you to participate at whatever depth of involvement you feel comfortable with while still benefiting from a connection with like-hearted Pagan individuals.

National-level organizations such as the Pagan Federation, Covenant of the Goddess, and Circle Sanctuary (to name just a few) can provide a way of staying informed on larger Pagan issues, such as political advocacy, and also provide legal-defense support regarding religious discrimination. They also host festivals and events that can be a great way to network with other Pagans. For example, Circle Sanctuary hosts an annual festival around Midsummer called Pagan Spirit Gathering that is attended by Pagans from all over the US and is filled with workshops, rituals, and vendors. Events such as these are great opportunities to fulfill that need for community while still remaining a solitary practitioner. They also provide access to teachers and leading voices in the community in the form of workshops and talks that can help you learn new skills, crafts, and information to help you make further progress in your spiritual practice.

Finding local groups to join can sometimes be a bit trickier. Despite the ever-growing number of Pagans, while it is almost guaranteed that you aren't the only Pagan in your area, established groups are harder to find outside of big cities. It can be especially difficult to find groups in every tradition outside of metropolitan areas. But a local group that isn't in an ideal tradition can still be a great way to connect with other Pagans. As they are the only Pagan option, it wouldn't be unusual to find Pagans who are interested in other traditions but craving involvement in a community. In this way, you can make connections and stay informed of new groups and other local events.

One way to find local Pagan groups can be to check bulletin-board listings at coffee shops, libraries, universities, and natural-food stores. It's definitely old-school, but these continue to be ways that groups and events are advertised. You can sometimes find related events, talks, and events happening in your area that are great learning opportunities, such as candle-making workshops, native-plant-identification walks, and talks on local folklore.

Naturally, the Internet is one of the best ways to find local groups and events, as well as information that you can apply in your practice. Local groups may have a website or be affiliated with Meetup.com. In many cities, the Autumn Equinox marks a time when Pagan Pride events are held. These are free and open to the public and can be a valuable way to connect with local Pagans. Often, local groups will have a table so they can talk with people and provide fliers and information about themselves. Pagan Pride events also tend to feature workshops, open rituals, and vendors, making them a great way to stretch your limbs as a new Pagan and begin exploring your local community.

Honoring Your Comfort

Even though you may find yourself drawn to Paganism, you may find that you aren't ready to fully commit to Pagan practice. You may have obligations and commitments that make it difficult to leave your current religion, or perhaps you have family members or partners who may not be supportive of you beginning to practice a different religion.

Each of us is responsible for making decisions for ourselves in our lives. While some religions place a heavy emphasis on believing the "right" things and behaving the "right" way, Paganism emphasizes your right to choose and the sacredness of your personal spiritual journey. Regardless of the level that you are comfortable with or at which you are able to be involved in Paganism, know that you are not cut off from the Pagan community. You are not without resources or people who are willing to talk with you and share their own experiences and information to help you figure out what is best for you and your spiritual path.

Although there is the possibility that, after much research and soul-searching, you decide that Paganism isn't the right choice for you, you are still welcome to reach out to Pagan individuals and communities to help you with your searching. While discernment is always advised when contacting or meeting new people, even online, approaching people and groups with respect and transparency regarding your searching can help you avoid misunderstandings while still finding the guidance you need. The Internet makes it especially easy to reach out at your convenience without any implied obligations on your side or for the people you contact.

Pagan Engagement

For many Pagans, environmental and social activism is a significant part of how they live their values and engage with the larger Pagan community. As Paganism is a collection of Earth-centric traditions, concern for the environment is a way for us to come together across traditions and work to help create change on a larger level. This common ground helps foster a greater sense of community and belonging, especially if you live in an area where finding Pagans of the same tradition can be difficult due to generally lower population levels. In this way, Pagans of greatly differing traditions are still able to benefit from fellowship with others through a focus on service projects, such as litter collection, habitat restoration, and volunteering with community-focused programs and nonprofit organizations.

This activism can take many other forms due to a shared view of the sacredness of the natural world. Within some Pagan groups, magick and ritual will frequently focus on environmental and social issues, with the group working together to raise and send out energy to encourage greater concern among others or to protect the land and at-risk individuals and peoples, for example. This magickal work is often done as an extension of everyday efforts, which may include educational work within the larger community.

Some larger Pagan organizations have formally rallied around these issues, actively working to educate and advocate. A prominent example is the founding of the Lady Liberty League by Circle Sanctuary, which is focused on maintaining religious freedom and providing civil support to Pagans through legal aid and advocacy. Circle Sanctuary itself is a leading Pagan organization in environmental preservation, headquartered in a nature preserve and containing one of the first green cemeteries in the US. Another example is the Covenant of the Goddess, an international organization of autonomous Wiccan groups, covens, and individuals focused on interfaith work, environmental activism, legal assistance regarding religious discrimination, and local community-based projects. Many regionally focused groups devoted to serving the Pagan community in connection with particular social issues also exist, such as the Appalachian Pagan Ministry, a volunteer-run organization serving incarcerated Pagans in about 20 prisons, including death row, in Ohio and West Virginia.

Outside of Pagan organizations, many Pagans, including solitaries, take a strong stance in regard to environmental and social issues, such as LGBTQIA+ and women's rights. More often than not, Pagans actively vote, reach out to legislators, and make changes in their lives that support their religious and spiritual values. They also engage with non-Pagan groups centered upon political and environmental issues, both on- and offline, to stay informed, discuss growing concerns, and identify ways to help.

Commitment to the Pagan value of freedom of choice means that despite these shared views regarding the environment and many social issues, Pagans espouse a variety of political views, ranging from conservative to green to libertarian to liberal. There is no one political stance that is more Pagan than another, and that's to the benefit of our religious community. Through this diversity of views, ideas, and experiences, our community is made stronger, and commitment to our shared values remains strong.

Continuing Your Journey

One of the most beautiful aspects of walking a Pagan path is the encouragement we each have to remain curious and always be searching. While other religions may focus on bending members around their ideal, Paganism asks that you determine what that ideal is for yourself and then provides you with the tools and community to help you get as close to that ideal as you can.

Your spiritual journey is just that—a *journey*. It is not a static point and certainly not a path taken in order to arrive at any particular destination. Rather, it is a series of experiences you have in traveling the path that unfolds before you. While you may not always know the direction you're headed, your path remains your own, stretching firmly behind you and informing every step you take as you move confidently forward. The details of how you travel that path will change. Your interests and spiritual needs will change and grow as you change and grow as a person. And this is exactly as it should be.

Your spiritual path is yours alone. No one can tell you what it should look like or what it should contain, and that remains true within Paganism regardless of whether you practice as an eclectic solitary or within a tradition. As Pagans, we are each responsible for finding our way, for focusing on spiritual growth, and for deepening our connection to the Earth and the Gods. Wherever your journey takes you, know that you walk with the energy of an entire community at your side, a community bound by a shared view of the inherent sacredness of the natural world and the value of living a life of spirituality.

Resources

Websites

Appalachian Pagan Ministry

www.appalachianpaganministry.com

A volunteer-based Pagan ministry largely focused on help-ing incarcerated Pagans secure their religious rights through in-person religious observance, counseling, and education, APM currently serves incarcerated Pagans in about 20 prisons throughout Ohio and West Virginia, making them one of the most extensive and active Pagan prison ministries in the United States.

Circle Sanctuary

www.circlesanctuary.org

One of the oldest legally recognized Wiccan organizations in the US, Circle Sanctuary is also a 200-acre nature preserve and has one of the first green cemeteries in the country. In addition to offering ministerial training and ordination, Circle Sanctuary hosts monthly events, workshops, and the annual Pagan Spirit Gathering, a weeklong festival that is one of the oldest and larg-est in the country.

Covenant of the Goddess

www.cog.org

An international organization of autonomous Wiccan covens and individuals, COG is largely focused on advocacy, working to support Wiccans and witches in protecting their religious rights, and on educating the public.

The Druid Network

www.druidnetwork.org

The only currently recognized Pagan charity in the UK, the Druid Network has a wealth of information on Druid practices and beliefs as well as providing networking opportunities.

Lady Liberty League

www.circlesanctuary.org/index.php/lady-liberty-league
/lady-liberty-league

Founded by Selena Fox of Circle Sanctuary, LLL is focused on preserving and defending religious freedom and civil rights through advocacy, education, networking, and legal defense.

The Pagan Federation

www.paganfed.org

The largest Pagan organization in the UK, the Pagan Federation provides networking opportunities as well as a plethora of information regarding Paganism and some Pagan traditions, notably Wicca, Druidry, Heathenry, and Shamanism.

PaganSquare

www.witchesandpagans.com

Attached to the *Witches & Pagans* magazine, PaganSquare is a blog space open to the community to post about and discuss topics relevant to Paganism and spiritual practice. Blogs are categorized for ease of searching and following topics of interest.

The Wild Hunt

www.wildhunt.org

The leading source for Pagan news and current events, featuring daily articles as well as weekly columns, the Wild Hunt covers world and local news relevant to Pagan interests and pertaining to issues that affect Pagans.

Books

Pagans and the Law: Understand Your Rights, by Dana D. Eilers
Written by an experienced US lawyer, this is the only book that looks at the legal standing of Pagans. Covering constitutional law, family law, employment law, landlord/tenant issues, and more, this is an essential book for American Pagan libraries.

The Triumph of the Moon: A History of Modern Pagan Witch-craft, by Ronald Hutton
While it focuses specifically on the rise of Pagan witchcraft, this book takes an in-depth look at prominent aspects of the history of modern Paganism, highlighting influences and trends, the involvement of prominent elders, and other notable factors to present a fuller context of the environment that allowed Paganism to take hold and flourish.

A World Full of Gods: An Inquiry into Polytheism, by John Michael Greer
This book is a thoughtful primer on the philosophy of religion with a focus on the philosophical case for a polytheistic understanding of the world along with ideas, themes, and concepts that are essential in understanding Pagan and polytheistic theology.

Glossary

altar: A flat surface used to hold religious items and tools, such as representations of deities, and a place to make offerings to deities and spirits. An altar may be erected as needed and taken down when not in use or left up permanently (making it more properly a *shrine*).

animism: A worldview holding that the world is alive with spirits and that all physical objects, both natural and man-made, contain a spirit with whom we are able to interact and communicate.

correspondence: The relationship between two things that allows the use of one as a means of tapping into the type of energy associated with the other (e.g., blue candles being used in healing magick because the color blue corresponds to healing energy).

coven: An organizational style with a distinct structure common to British Traditional Wicca and other witch traditions and groups. Covens typically number no more than 13 members and feature a hierarchical structure of three degrees, with two members of the highest degree leading and organizing the coven. Leadership is static.

deity: A spiritual being of significant power and influence Who is able to effect changes within our lives as easily as They are able to effect changes in the physical world and the spirit world.

divination: A collection of techniques for interpreting spiritual forces that provides us with additional information so we can make better-informed decisions in our lives, as well as helping us learn more about ourselves, the world, and the Gods and spirits with Whom we engage.

dualism: A worldview based upon clear separation between humans and deities as well as between the physical world and the spirit world, a separation prevents humans from personally engaging with deities and the spirit world. Dualism holds the physical to be inferior to the spiritual and is incompatible with Paganism. Dualism is typically found within monotheistic religions.

Earth-centric: A term denoting the view that value is inherent to the natural world. Paganism views the Earth and all the physical world as sacred and the Gods as the movers and shakers of all the worlds.

energy: A common term to describe spiritual forces that are believed to be within all things as well as moving outside of all things independently. Energy can be raised (that is, gathered or tapped into) and directed as part of magick and spell work. This is not the same energy as described in various scientific fields.

magick: The action of using spiritual forces to create change. There are numerous magickal systems, such as ceremonial magic and witchcraft, that take different approaches to working magick as well as differing in their overall goal for the use of magick.

monotheism: A worldview holding that there exists only one deity. It is frequently accompanied by *dualism*, the view that there exists separation between humans and that deity.

moot: Originally British slang for a casual get-together. The international nature of the Pagan community (especially online) means that this word is commonly used by Pagans for any casual meeting, such as "Pagan Night Out."

offering: Anything given as a gift of gratitude and honor to the Gods or a spirit. Offerings may be objects (such as food, candles, handicrafts, etc.), or they may be actions (such as song, dance, energy work, charity work, etc.).

Paganism: A modern religious movement encompassing many different traditions with a shared modern history. Paganism is distinguished by a lack of central governing institutions and religious hierarchy, as well as a fundamentally different worldview from that of dominant Western religions. Paganism places importance on the natural world, the right of individual choice, the strength of a diverse community, and a definition of membership based on action—not belief.

panentheism: A worldview that holds that there is a divine force that exists within all things as well as simultaneously existing outside of (and separate from) those things. This divine force is impersonal, largely unknowable, and generally unconcerned with humans on an individual level. Compare with *pantheism*.

pantheism: A worldview that holds that there is a divine force that exists within all things. This divine force is impersonal, unknowable, and generally unconcerned with humans. Compare with *panentheism*.

polytheism: A worldview affirming the existence of many individual and unique deities with Whom humans are able to engage and Who are very active within the physical world and the spirit world alike.

ritual: A common term for religious services, gatherings, or observances. A ritual can be devotional and/or magickal and can be performed alone or in a group.

Sabbat: The general name for any of the eight holidays that make up the Wheel of the Year.

spirit: A category of beings that exist in energetic form and may or may not also possess a physical form. Many spirits are purely energetic and may not have ever been physically incarnate. As a category, the term *spirit* can refer to the animating consciousness within plants and stones, the residual personality and substance of a departed human or animal, and deities, as well as a number of spiritual beings that have never been and will never be corporeal.

spirit worker: A religious specialist who serves the community by acting as an intermediary between the physical world and the spirit world. They may provide services such as divination, spiritual healing, and Oracular work, as well as sometimes providing clergy services such as officiating weddings and handfastings or providing spiritual counseling.

spiritism or spiritualism: The belief that humans are able to communicate and interact with the spirits of the dead and, therefore, there is a continuity of the person that presupposes and transcends death.

tradition: One of the numerous separate religions that Paganism as a religious movement is comprised of. These traditions are unique, frequently honoring different pantheons of deities and having different ritual formats.

Wheel of the Year: The collective name for eight holidays known as *Sabbats* and found within eclectic Paganism and specifically within Wicca, as well as being followed by some Druids, Heathens, and Pagan witches.

witchcraft: A magickal system that emphasizes creating change in the everyday and is defined by its fundamental basis in animism, divination, herbalism, the land, ritual, and spirit work. It is not inherently religious but can to be practiced with or without any religious context. It is prominent within Paganism.

REFERENCES

American Religious Identification Survey. "Self-Described Religious Identification of Adult Population: 1990 to 2008." U.S. Census Bureau, Statistical Abstract of the United States: 2011, table 75. Accessed October 19, 2019. https://www2.census.gov/library/publications/2010/compendia/statab/130ed/tables/11s0075.pdf.

Berger, Helen A. 2019. *Solitary Pagans: Contemporary Witches, Wiccans, and Others Who Practice Alone*. Columbia: University of South Carolina Press.

Berger, Helen A., Evan A. Leach, and Leigh S. Shaffer. 2003. *Voices from the Pagan Census: A National Survey of Witches and Neo-Pagans in the United States*. Studies in Comparative Religion, ed. Frederick M. Denny. Columbia: University of South Carolina Press.

Office of National Statistics. "2011 Census in England and Wales: Written Answers to the 'What is Your Religion?' Question." Accessed October 19, 2019. https://webarchive.nationalarchives.gov.uk/20160310054508/http://visual.ons.gov.uk/infographic-what-is-your-religion/.

Pew Research Center. "2014 Religious Landscape Study, RLS-II." Accessed October 19, 2019. https://www.pewforum.org/religious-landscape-study/.

ReligiousTolerance. "The Number of Wiccans in the U.S. during 2015 to 2018: It May Be the Second Largest Theistic Faith Group; the Fastest Growing in Terms of Percentage: Part 7." Accessed October 19, 2019. http://www.religioustolerance.org/estimated-number-of-wiccans-in-the-united-states-7.htm/.

INDEX

ACKNOWLEDGMENTS

Hail and rejoice then, Leto the blessèd, for
glorious children

you bore, lordly Apollo and Artemis shooter of arrows,

her in Ortygia, him brought forth in Delos the rocky,

while you reclined on a great tall peak of the
Kynthian highland,

close to a date-palm tree by the streams of the
River Inópos.

How shall I sing of you who are in all ways worthy
of singing?

—Homeric Hymn 3, lines 14–19

ABOUT THE AUTHOR

 **ALTHAEA SEBASTIANI** is a spirit worker, author, and spirit-led witch with 25 years of experience, and dedicated priestess to Divine Twins who keep her life full and interesting. Her practice is land-based and devotional, focused on being responsive to the spirits of the land wherever her travels take her and doing right by the Gods who have called her into Their service. When not writing, throwing the bones, or cavorting with Gods and spirits, Althaea spends her time wrangling six half-feral children with her husband, wandering about the West in a tiny traveling house, and living off-grid in the wilderness. Find her on social media @LadyAlthaea or at www.ladyalthaea.com.